Colophon

Photography and concept	Jan Bartelsman
Marketing, sales and project management	Aliya Hallim-Byne of Aliyan
Cover design	Ruparo Amsterdam
Graphic design	Peter Koomen
Layout	Fotostudio Jan Bartelsman BV: Yasmin Danenberg, Monique Borgmann
Printing	Toppan Printing Company America Inc. www.ta.toppan.com
Publisher	Fotostudio Jan Bartelsman BV The Netherlands tel. +31 (0)228-58 41 67 jan@bartelsman.nl www.bartelsman.nl
Editor	Colleen Mastrovaselis
Translation and editing:	Sherrill Rose
With thanks to	All participating restaurants, Astrid Meester, Marisa Perry, Douglas Elliott, Tom Rietveld, Ronald Huiskamp, Emma Curtis, Marjorie Schulman, David Barrington, Eddy Creces, Nicolas Mazard, Jim Snyder, Eveline, Boris, Julian and Nina Bartelsman, Hannah and A.M. Hallim
ISBN	978-90-74108-44-7
NUR	504

Table of Contents

Restaurant index

Preface

'These vagabond shoes are longing to stray …'
Like so many people, I sometimes think that song was written for me. And like so many people, I love New York. That's why, when I realized how long it had been since I had visited this great city, I decided to do something about it. And even before I stepped onto the plane, I knew something special was going to happen.

And it did. Sometimes you just happen to be in the right place at the right time. The right place and time came for me one morning as I was running across the Williamsburg Bridge. Sometimes you get those moments when running, when everything magically falls into place. I suddenly knew that I had to find a way to spend more time in New York. As a culinary photographer, what could be better for me than to start working on a book about the great chefs of New York? I finished my run, took a hot shower, and immediately started phoning the 'big guys'.

Making this "best chefs" edition was a tricky thing to do. How can one know who the best chefs are? Relying on existing guide books and magazines that award points and stars can get you started, but is it 100% reliable? I wasn't averse to the idea of having dinner at all the restaurants in question to find out, but that turned out to be impractical. We came up with the next best thing: we arranged photo shoots of the culinary creations of the "top notch" chefs we had heard and read about. We asked them to prepare their dishes to taste, which is not usually the case in food photography, lamentably. We reckoned that if the food was good, it should get a place in our book. And guess what? We didn't have to kick a single restaurant out of the book!

Thank you, chefs and restaurateurs. Thank you, writers!

Jan Bartelsman

Discerning taste

Enjoy and... turn the tide

In food circles, one frequently hears that everything tasted better in Grandma's day, and although the remark is often dismissed as cliché, like most clichés, it contains a kernel of truth. Cookbooks written by celebrity chefs often contain passages describing their outings with Granny to forage for wild berries. The taste of the resulting cakes and pies is forever imprinted on the chefs' memories. And Granny's stew, which simmered on the stovetop for hours and hours, sent its lovely aroma wafting through the house and across the years.

Let's say that things did taste better in bygone days... this means that things taste worse today, and that is a tough nut to swallow. It is also a remarkable state of affairs in our western economy, which is so eager to cater to consumers' tastes. Indeed, many aficionados of food and drink lament the ongoing trends of the last few decades that have resulted in the diminishing of genuine flavors.

In the last few years, the culinary world has mounted a frontal attack on the trend towards diminishing flavors. Concerned chefs are waging personal crusades against the demise of Genuine Flavor.

The "Slow Food" movement taking the world by storm is particularly concerned with the issue of Flavor. Proponents of "slow-food" are trying to establish a Flavor Ark, a sort of Noah's Ark to preserve flavors, to save them from extinction (www.slowfood.com).

What is going on here? What do we mean by "diminishing flavors"? How does it happen, and what can we do about it? Culinary books and magazines point an accusing finger at commerce. Terms such as food industry, globalization, fast-food chains, convenience foods and factory farming are bandied about with growing frequency. It is easy to conclude that these relatively new phenomena are pushing traditional flavors and dishes onto the back burner, but when we consider the issue more closely, we can see that the reality of the situation is more complicated than that.

In trying to determine what diminishing flavor is, we quickly arrive at the question: what is flavor? One important issue to be raised is the distinction between flavor and taste, i.e., flavor that is characteristic to a particular product, and the way that we, as consumers, experience the taste of those flavors. The diminishing of flavor, then, can mean many things: that products have less flavor, that people have a diminished capacity to taste, that we are content with less flavor, or that we simply have developed a sense of "bad taste."

With regard to a product's diminishing flavor, there are several things to consider. To begin with, the food industry prepares many consumer foods using artificial flavors, colors and preservatives, not to mention sweeteners, sugar and salt. The result of this phenomenon is that people are less and less able to taste levels of saltiness and sweetness, and therefore consume unhealthy levels of both. Another issue has to do with methods of mass production, during which the authentic flavors and delicate aromas of many products are simply lost.

The average tomato and nectarine may differ more from one another in appearance than they do in flavor. A factory-farmed chicken filet may be described as follows: Taste? Erased. Compensation for the dull flavors of such products – and this is especially so with pre-prepared dishes – often comes in the form of added sweeteners and salt.

Wild Salmon   **Factory farmed Salmon**

In this way, the original flavors of the products are less discernible, and we wind up with a diverse array of products that taste more and more alike.

And so we come full circle: Lack of flavor leads to salt and sugar overkill, which in turn dulls our taste buds and makes us more accepting of flavorless products. It is the age-old conundrum of the chicken and the egg.

But that's not all. Whoever says that "diminishing flavor" is exclusively a matter of culinary degeneration, and whoever thinks that "taste" can be pure and unsullied, probably doesn't have any kids. The predilection of children from all corners of the globe for sickeningly sweet ices with artificial colors and flavors points not only to an absence of survival instinct, but also of good taste. Parents go to absurd lengths in order to coax a few veggies into pint-sized mouths. My children prefer a deep-fried chicken nugget from the local fast food chain to a grilled steak from a locally raised, clover-grazed cow, lovingly grilled by yours truly on our barbecue.

There has been much speculation as to the cause of this logic-defying situation. Mother's milk, which is naturally sweet, is singled out by some as a culprit, leading children to develop a fondness for sweet things. Others point to the fact that children's taste buds are not fully developed, and that they have a natural aversion to products with strong flavors such as sauerkraut and wild game. According to this theory, children are naturally inclined towards foods with duller flavors, but then, that leads one to wonder about their love of extreme sweetness.

In any case, the food industry has certainly taken an interest in the multitudes of young consumers over the past couple of decades. The industry takes children's likes and dislikes very seriously, and more and more products are targeted at this consumer group. Marketing is a handy tool with this age group, as is illustrated by fast food chain, MacDonald's. Children are especially vulnerable to the fantasy worlds that are brought to them by marketers and advertisers. Packaging alone can easily lead them to choose and prefer a factory product to its natural counterpart. Shortly, the younger generation is at risk of never learning to know and value good, "old-fashioned" flavors.

Happily, the tide is turning.

More and more people are now discovering how delicious "genuinely flavorful" food can be. Flavorful products are at the root of this discovery. And whether the food is being prepared at home or in haute-cuisine restaurants, "genuinely flavorful" means: high-quality basic products.

The chefs of the restaurants in this book devote much care and energy to the selection of their ingredients. They are committed to using as many local, seasonal vegetables, fruits, meats and dairy products as they can. They do this simply because such products are intensely flavorful. The dishes they prepare with these products are often so delicious that customers rave about them.

I have experienced this first-hand. I thought that green asparagus was essentially flavorless until I tasted a simple dish, asparagus with hollandaise sauce, prepared by a discerning chef. I was flabbergasted. It was as though I were eating asparagus for the first time in my life: delightful! It turned out that the asparagus had just been harvested a few hours previously, a couple of miles down the road! They were bursting with flavor. Asparagus from farther afield – out of season, it is flown in from Africa – simply cannot be fresh by definition.

Such is the case with many vegetables and fruits: the flavor wanes with each hour following its harvest. For this reason alone local and seasonal products often have more flavor than those made for mass consumption. The origins of dairy, meat and fish products can also affect levels of flavor in these products.

Experienced chefs know that the best place to find quality products is in their own region, at local farms, and in season. That's why the food we get in their restaurants is so enjoyable. But we can serve up the same delicious fare at home if we make the effort to go out and find the best ingredients.

In this way, the solution to the problem of "diminishing flavor" is surprisingly simple. Simply enjoy good food! The demand for quality ingredients will grow and high-quality, locally produced goods will become more easily available. And the cycle of "diminishing flavor" will be broken.

Another great advantage to this situation is that flavorful products are often not just better for our health, they are also better for the health of the natural world, animals and the environment. The best example of this is perhaps the farm-fresh egg produced by a free-range chicken fed on farm-fresh grains and greens. The difference between this egg and the lackluster egg produced by a chicken confined to a miserable existence in a battery cage is enormous: the farm fresh egg is characterized by the deep color of its yolk, the strength of its shell and the intensity of its flavor.

Factory farming is not just a flavor-killer; it also causes damage to the environment. One of the less well-known, more shocking, consequences of factory farming is its threat to the world's fish stocks. The seas are being depleted of fish, mainly to supply fishmeal to the factory farming industry. It is then made into feed for both "wet" factory farming installations (seafood) and "dry" factory farming installations (land animals). This is the single largest threat to the existence of sea life as a whole.

When you purchase local products, this, too, is less taxing for the environment. Long Island Free Range Duck, Peconic Bay Oysters and John Codzallas Asparagus require fewer food miles than products that are flown in from faraway places. This also holds true for fruits and vegetables.

That animals belong in the group of "flavorful" local products is also becoming increasingly evident. Locally produced cheese made from free-range sheep-, cow- or goat- milk tastes better than cheese produced from the milk of animals that are kept shut up in stalls. The grass on which they graze is a contributing factor in the character of the cheese produced. Many, high-quality, flavorful regional products are grown in the New York area. (Handy address list at the back of the book!)

It is my great wish that my children learn to enjoy good food with genuine flavor. Learning to eat well is an important part of their upbringing, but this is not easily achieved: I believe that for them, just as for myself, enjoyment of the food they eat should be at the top of the list. So when I see how excited they get when they are asked to go with friends to Mickey-D's, I still feel rather depressed.

I try to let them be seduced by my own enthusiasm for what I am eating, in the hope that they will be tempted to try it, and like it. I also enjoy taking them to good restaurants like the ones represented in this book. In the end, they are the best weapons in the crusade against "diminishing flavor."

I am optimistic.

Jan Bartelsman
In collaboration with Janse Schöttelndreiër.

Sources:

Peter Klosse
Het Proefboek – De essentie van smaak
(The Book of Taste: Essential Flavors), Tirion, Baarn, 2003

Wouter Klootwijk
De Goede Visgids – Vis eten met goed geweten
(The Good Fish Guide: Eating Fish with a Good Conscience),
Schuyt & Co., Utrecht, 2004

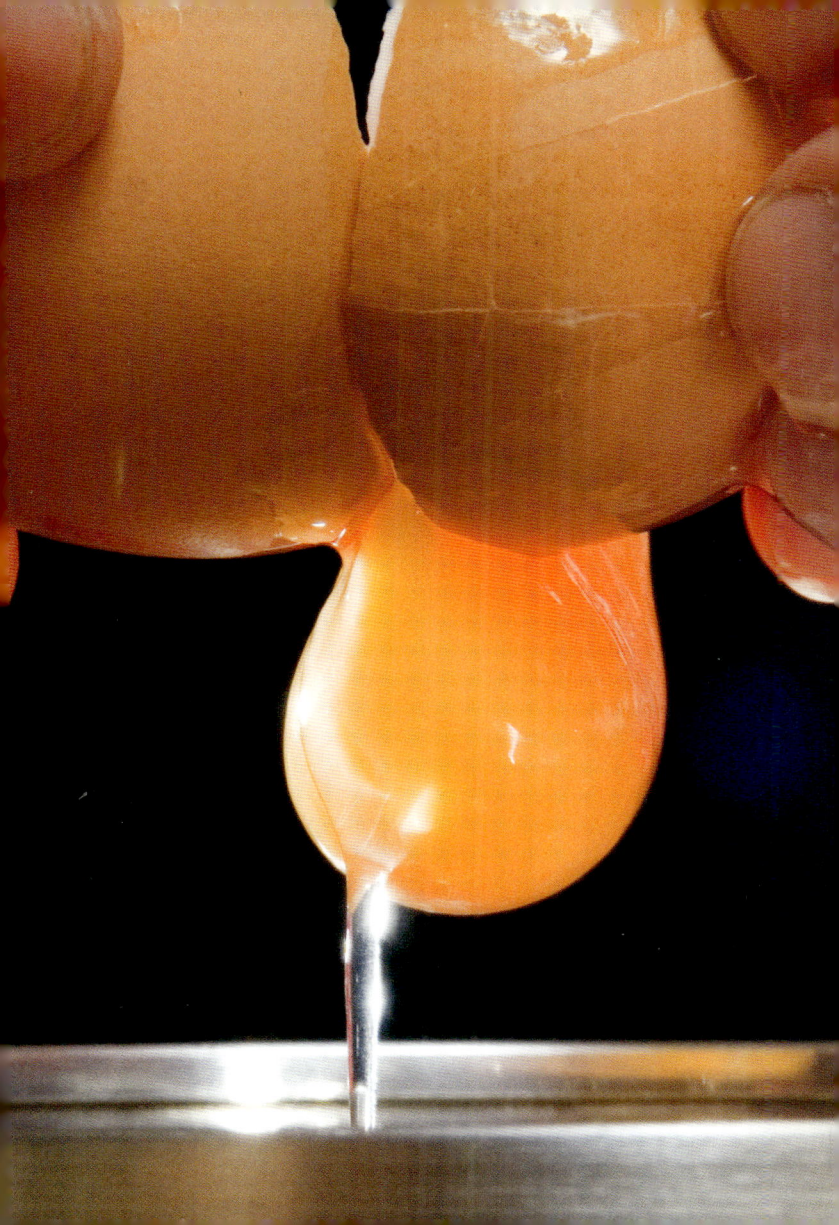

Annisa
13 Barrow Street (Between 7th avenue and West 4th Street)

Annisa

Address: 13 Barrow Street, New York, NY 10014
(Between 7th avenue and West 4th Street)
Phone: (212) 741 6699
Internet: www.annisarestaurant.com

Cuisine: Contemporary American

Owners: Anita Lo (Chef) and Jennifer Scism (Sommelier and GM)

Business hours: 5:30PM - 10:30PM, Sunday 5:30PM - 9:30PM

Private dining: Entire dining room available. Maximum 48.

Payment: All major credit cards

Price: $75 and up per person

Ratings: 1 Michelin Star, Zagat: Food 27, Service 26

Reservations: Recommended, *Dress Code:* Business Casual

Interior Design: Jennifer Scism

Notable features: Almost all wines on the unique list are either made by female vintners and/or made at vineyards with female proprietors. Chef Anita Lo has been named one of ten "Best New Chefs in America" by Food and Wine magazine as well as "Best New Restaurant Chef" by the Village Voice.

From top left to bottom right:
• Skate with Avocado and Radishes, Korean Flavors
• Duck and Buckwheat Ochazuke
• Tuna with Three Mints
• Poppyseed Bread and Butter Pudding with Meyer Lemon Curd

Anthos
36 West 52nd Street (between 5th and 6th Avenues)

Anthos

Address: 36 West 52nd Street, New York, NY 10019
(between 5th and 6th Avenues)
Phone: (212) 582 6900, *Fax:* (212) 245 5211
Internet: www.anthosnyc.com

Cuisine: New Greek

Owners: Donatella Arpaia and Michael Psilakis

Business hours: 12:00PM - 2:45PM, 5:00PM - 10.30PM,
Sat and Sun: 5:00PM - 11.00PM, Closed Sunday, No lunch Saturday

Executive Chef: Michael Psilakis

Press Contact: Bullfrog & Baum, Katherine Bryant, (212) 255 6717
mail to: katherine@bullfrogandbaum.com or olga@bullfrogandbaum.com

Payment: Amex, Mastercard, Visa, Diners

Price: Appetizers $17 - $20, Entrees $28 - $38, Dessert $9 - $12
Prix-Fixe Lunch

Private events: Semi Private Room Upstairs seats 12
Full Private Room Upstairs seats 20, Pre-Theatre Prix-Fixe

Ratings: 1 Michelin Star, Zagat: Food 25, Service 21

Reservations: up to one month in advance, *Dress Code:* business casual

Interior Design: Matthew Sudock of M Design

Notable features: Greek, French, American and Italian wine
between $35-$2000.

From top left to bottom right:
- Raw Meze: Kampachi, Fluke, Tuna, Salmon, Hamachi
- Goat Pastitsio: feta Macaronia, lobster mushroom, seared green olive,
  scallion, mustard green
- Smoked Octopus: fennel yogurt, celery, fennel, pickled onion,
  marinated mushroom
- Swordfish Spetsofai: loukanico sausage, lemon cucumber, pickled chili,
  onion confit, caper, basil, sweet chili broth

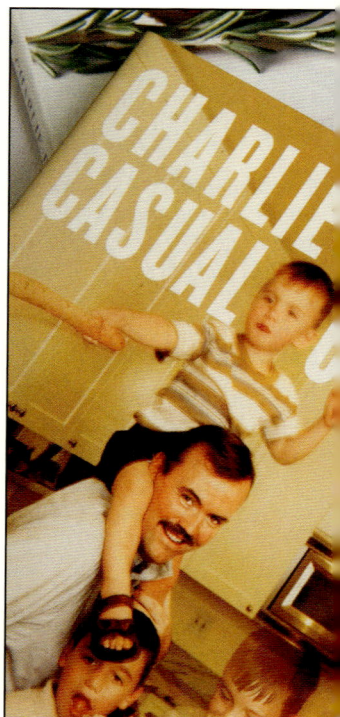

Aureole
34 East 61st Street (As of April 2009: 1 Bryant Park)

THE ART OF AUREOLE

Aureole

Address: 34 East 61st Street New York, NY 10065
(Between Madison and Park Avenues)
After April 2009: 1 Bryant Park
Phone: (212) 319 1660, *Fax:* (212) 750 8613
Internet: www.charliepalmer.com

Cuisine: Progressive American

Chef-Owner: Charlie Palmer, *Executive Chef:* Tony Aiazzi

Business hours: 5:30PM - 11:00PM, Sat 5:00PM - 11:00PM
Closed Sundays

General Manager: Charles Pouchot

Wine Director: Justin Lorenz, *Pastry Chef:* Rachel Lansing-Hidalgo

Groups: (max group size): 30

Prix Fixe: $ 84

Payment: All major credit cards

Ratings: 1 Michelin Star, Zagat: Food 27, Service 25

Reservations: Recommended

Dress Code: Casual Elegant

Interior Design: Adam D. Tihany

Parking: parking garage across the street

Additional Features: Stunning Wine Display, Member of Re'ais & Chateaux

From top left to bottom right:
- Sauteed Soft Shelled Crab with Red Jalapeno and
  Mango soy lime vinaigrette, scallions
- Pan Roasted Halibut with Summer Vegetable Saute
  sweet pea coulis, tarragon crust
- Grilled Beef Rib-Eye with Phyllo Crisped Oysters
  wild mushrooms, baby spinach
- Dark Chocolate Amaretto Bread Pudding
  warm cherry compote, sour cherry sorbet

The tracks of my tours: Farmer's market

Most people react the same way to the farmers markets on my NYC culinary walking tours (see www.LizYoungTours.com). Upon seeing the stacked rows of bright and bursting produce, fresh cut flowers and herbs, stinky artisan cheeses or locally harvested honey, smiles widen and an enthusiasm envelopes the group. This may be a predisposed reaction, triggered after millennia of farming and eating, but it is unmistakable.

On the tours, we might run into one of the gifted chefs represented in this book, who long have relied on the Greenmarket farmers for supplies of high-quality, raw ingredients. Chefs can share the glory with the farmers, some of whom spend hours loading their trucks and hauling their bounty to NYC at least four times a week, then man their stalls for eight hours and drive back home to get back to the tasks on the farm.

Farmers' markets, once common throughout the city, were centralized and institutionalized in the beginning of the 19th century. However, after the centralized markets were disbanded or moved in the mid-1950s, many New Yorkers had only rotting produce to pick from on the market shelves.

Then, in 1976, the Council for the Environment began running the Greenmarkets – with only 12 farmers. Today, hundreds of farmers in the surrounding six states participate and help honor the goals: to preserve open space and provide fresh, local food.

Between 1994 and 2004, the number of farmers' markets doubled across the country to 3,706. Today, NYC leads with the largest Greenmarket network, having almost 50. And reports tout how 86 cents of every dollar spent there goes to the farmers rather than to middlemen distributors.

The Greenmarkets also help safeguard what is left of our area's biodiversity, and we need it! We lost 75% of our agricultural genetic diversity in the last century and so applaud these farmers for saving our vital resource of food. Some offer organic foods with 40% higher nutrient values and 2/3 less pesticide residue than foods synthetically locations, the Greenmarket connects those who still may not have fresh, local produce options in their own neighborhood stores.

As we walk through the crowded stalls, I explain the benefits of buying at the Greenmarket and the seasonally progressive offerings. Almost all are produced within 200 miles of the city, as the rules demand.

Although the market continues all year, the real show in the Northeast begins in spring with, among other things, shell beans, new greens and Jerusalem artichokes in April. May offers rhubarb, asparagus and fiddle head ferns. My favorites in June are the fennel, peas and cherries. It's hard to pick favorites as the summer heightens (tomatoes? corn? berries? apricots?) and the market stands overflow with choices for the 60,000 peak day shoppers.

I talk expectantly about the corn from Sycamore Farms and we taste the fresh, salt-covered pretzels from Martin's. I politely snap off a French Breakfast radish from Migliorelli's farm to share before we purchase some to take home.

We discuss Morse Pitts, the farmer/owner of Windfall Farms, who helped promote the "certified organic" classification and then refused to use it. For him, the rules that govern the right to use the term became warped during the law-making process and so he no longer espouses it.

On Wednesdays, we visit Château Renaissance's stand, where French owner, Patrice DeMay, offers tastings of the wines he crafts in NY's Finger Lakes using his family's 400-year-old recipes. I'm sure to highlight Elly Hushour's goat cheese or S&SO's produce grown in rich, Orange County black dirt and the owner, Stanley Osczepinski, one of the market's first farmers.

Walking through, it's hard to avoid the vibrancy in the Greenmarket system in NYC. And it's hard not to smile, just like my tour-goers.

Liz Young, www.LizYoungTours.com

Babbo
110 Waverly Place (Between MacDougal and 6th Avenue)

Babbo

Address: 110 Waverly Place, New York, NY 10011
(Between Macdougal and Sixth Avenue)
Phone: (212) 777 0303, *Fax:* (212) 777 3365
Internet: www.babbonyc.com

Cuisine: Italian

Owners: Mario Batali & Joseph Bastianich

Business hours: 5:30PM - 11:30PM, Sun 5:00PM - 11.00PM

Closed: (Vacation) Thanksgiving Day And Christmas Day

General Manager: Colum Sheehan

Executive Chef: Frank Langello

Pastry chef: Gina Depalma

Maître d': John Mainieri

Wine Director: Luca Pasquinelli

Groups (max. group size): 6 people

Payment: Amex, Mastercard, Visa, Diners ALL

Price: $75 and up

Ratings: 1 Michelin Star, Zagat: Food 27, Service 25

Reservations: one month in advance

Dress Code: casual smart

Additional features: wheelchair accessible, James Beard Foundation's Best
New Restaurant Award for 1998.

From top left to bottom right:
• Roasted Beet Tartare with Chianti Vinegar and Ricotta Salata
• Black Spaghetti with Rock Shrimp, Spicy Salami Calabrese and Green Chiles
• Fennel Dusted Sweetbreads with Sweet and Sour Onions, Duck Bacon
  and Membrillo Vinegar
• Pistachio and Chocolate Semifreddo

Blue Hill
75 Washington Place (Between Washington Square Park and 6th Avenue)

Blue Hill

Address: 75 Washington Place
(Between Washington Square Park and 6th Avenue)
Phone: (212) 539 1776, *Fax:* (212) 539 0959
Internet: www.bluehillfarm.com

Cuisine: seasonal american

Executive Chef and Co-Owner: Dan Barber

Owners: David and Laureen Barber

Business hours: 5:30PM - 11:00PM, Sun 5.30PM - 10.00PM

Closed: New Year's Day, Memorial Day, July 4th, Thanksgiving,
Christmas Eve and Christmas Day

General Manager: Franco Serafin

Wine Director: Claire Paparazzo

Groups (max. group size): 6

Private Dining: by special arrangement only; up to 16 guests

Payment: Amex, Mastercard, Visa, Diners

Food Ratings: 1 Michelin Star, 26 Zagat, Food, 3 stars New York Times

Service Ratings: 25 Zagat Service

Reservations: strongly recommended

Dress Code: casual elegant (cell phones and flash photography
discouraged in the dining room)

Architecture: Peter Guzy, of Asfour Guzy Architects

Interior Design: Laureen Barber

From top left to bottom:
- Spring Salad, raw and marinated vegetables, purslane and
  Blue Hill Farm Yogurt
- "Floating Island" Rhubarb, Tapioca Pudding
- Vegetables on a Fence

Alginato

Ferran Adrià, the internationally famous Spanish chef, has introduced the world to a host of new cooking techniques. One of these is called "Spherification." Using this technique, a chef combines alginato with vegetable or fruit juice; this mixture goes on to be encapsulated in caviar-like "spheres" that can be consumed like, well, caviar. Alginato is a seaweed extract and can be purchased in powder form. A gelling agent (calcium chloride) gives the "caviar" spheres a membrane. To show how the technique works, here is a simplified version of the basic recipe created by Ferran Adrià:

Melon caviar
5 dl cold water
2 g alginato
2½ g calcium chloride
250 g melon juice

Mix the alginato with a third of the melon juice. Then add the rest of the melon juice and stir until all of the alginato has dissolved into the fluid. Let the mixture rest for one hour. Dissolve the calcium chloride in the cold water. Using a syringe, release droplets of the melon juice mixture one by one into the calcium chloride. Allow the melon spheres to rest for one minute, then rinse them through a sieve. (For more information: www. texturaselbulli.com)

This technique is "hot" in the upper echelons of the gastronomic world. This makes sense when you consider that top chefs have to distinguish themselves from the rank and file, and therefore search for techniques that the hobbyist or brasserie chef wouldn't normally undertake. Introducing molecular gastronomy into restaurant kitchens has another fine advantage. Technical advance leads to a whole range of low-calorie dishes with enhanced flavors, from no-cream chocolate mousse to French fries that have been pre-soaked in a 3% salt solution. These fries contain 30% less fat than fries prepared the old-fashioned way, and guess what? They taste better. That, of course, is what it is all about!

Maarten van der Jagt

Customers

Regular customers. Without them we could never have made it so far, and not just professionally, but also in our personal lives. We have a regular following that has stayed with us over the years, sticking by us through thick and thin, and they continue to come back. Even so, the topic of customers remains a challenging factor in our world, and it is worthy of special consideration. Each and every customer deserves special handling. Day in and day out, we enter the fray in hope of a victory, but we are not in command of the customer's mood and frame of mind. One customer may be bothered by professional worries, another is trying to save a marriage; some are madly in love and have eyes only for each other, and some others are feeling prickly and are in a mood to regard everything with a critical eye. In the end, they must all receive the star treatment that leaves them feeling special.

Today's restaurant clientele is savvy; people dine out frequently and have a considerable store of dining experience that can be used for purposes of comparison. It's a pity, actually, because like proverbial apples and oranges, each restaurant has its own philosophy, its own style and its own tastes. The particular character of an individual restaurant will naturally impact on its product. A convivial atmosphere in the kitchen and dining room will result in working and dining pleasure. The chef and server weighed down by worries associated with things like costly renovations run the risk of allowing such cares to affect everything and everyone in the work environment, including the general atmosphere. If something goes wrong or the customer is having an off night, the restaurant may get the blame. What can we do about this? If you ask me, there is only one option: give it your double down-and-dirty best.

Thérèse Boer is co-author of many books on food and wine, and, with her husband Jonnie Boer, is co-owner of three-star Michelin Restaurant and Hotel "The Librije" in the Netherlands. www.librije.com

Bouley
163 Duane Street, Corner of Duane and Hudson Streets

Bouley

Address: 163 Duane Street, New York, NY 10013
(Corner of Duane and Hudson)
Phone: (212) 964 2525, *Fax:* (212) 693 7490
Internet: www.davidbouley.com

Cuisine: French

Chef-Owner: David Bouley, General Manager: Jay Futch

Business hours: 11:30AM - 3:00PM and 5:30PM - 12:00PM

Pastry Chef: Octavio Reyes, Head Sommelier: Olivier Dufeu

Private dining: Up to 60

Payment: Amex, Mastercard, Visa

Pricing: Around $90

Ratings: 2 Michelin Stars, Zagat: Food 28, Service 26, NY Times: 3 stars

Reservations: Recommended

Dress Code: Jacket Required

Designer: David Bouley

Additional features: Numerous

From top left to bottom:
- Organic Connecticut Farm Egg Steamed with Black Truffle, Serrano Ham, Parmesan Reggiano and 25-Year Old Balsamic Vinegar
- Tea-Smoked Organic Breast of Long Island Duckling with Truffle Honey Vanilla Glaze and a Balinese Peppercorn Crust, Oregon Rhubarb, Green Almonds, Chanterelle Mushrooms, Fava Beans, and Hawaiian Heart of Palm Purée
- Hot Valrhona Chocolate Soufflé, Vermont Maple Ice Cream, Vanilla Ice Cream and Chocolate Sorbet

Choosing the right spot

Where do you go when you want to have a "good meal"? Well, what do you mean by a "good meal"? And what it is for? Do you want plain or fancy? Comfort food or exotic culinary adventures? Glassware glittering on the table or will plastic utensils do? An intimate setting or a boisterous bistro? Candles or strobe lights? Sweet melodies or pulsating rock? A starched white table cloth with elaborately folded napkins or a formica table with paper all the way? A drop-dead view or a dark hideaway? A fashionable dining hour or the early bird special? (Me, I don't do noise, so quiet is at the top of my list.)

Make your own list, and you'll see why choosing the right spot is fraught with so much angst. Of course, what is most important changes based on the occasion, our moods, the company we'll keep, and on and on. How can any source tell us where to eat?

But we never give up hope that they will. We consult obsessively – from newspaper columns, journal reviews and guidebooks to idiosyncratic blogs. Do we seek a voice we know? Then we'll check out the regular critic for the *Times* or *New York Magazine* or the *New York Post* or the latest blog. These judges are paid to be opinionated, and we know to take their advice with a grain or three of salt, unless experience tells us that a given critic's judgment is likely to be ours as well.

Shouldn't we listen to our fellow diners? *Zagat's* tallies its votes and offers observations (some quite outrageous). Isn't this democracy in action, as *Zagat's* claims? Surely, all those people who frequent Starbucks aren't there just for WIFI.

But perhaps counting votes is not the answer for our dining dilemma. Is there no gold standard? The Michelin Guide comes as close to an impersonal system of evaluation as the culinary world offers. Its anonymous inspectors are the very opposite of judges or voters. Their ratings, they assure us, reflect a professional understanding of culinary achievement, unswayed by the emotions of the moment.

Yet it is precisely the connection of those emotions and those moments that makes a meal "great." So, anxious omnivores that we are, we check the papers and journals, scan *Zagat's*, check out some blogs, and take a look at Michelin. And then, just to be sure that the meal will be right for *us* on *this* occasion, we take one last step. For we want a recommendation that caters to *our* taste, *our* dreams and *our* desires, not to mention our pocketbook. And, in the end, since food talk is, still and all, word of mouth, just to be extra sure, after all our research online and off, we turn to a foodie friend. What will *I* like? Are you sure that it's right for *me*?

Priscilla Parkhurst Ferguson

Café Boulud
20 East 76th Street (Between Madison and Fifth Avenues)

Café Boulud

Address: 20 East 76th Street, New York, NY 10021
(Between Madison and Fifth Avenues)
Phone: (212) 772 2600, *Fax:* (212) 772 7755
Internet: www.danielnyc.com

Cuisine: French-American Cuisine inspired by Daniel Boulud's four muses:
Traditional, Seasonal, Vegetarian & World Cuisine

Chef-Owner: Daniel Boulud

Business hours: 12:00PM - 2:30PM, 5:45PM - 11:00PM,
No Sat lunch in July & Aug, Sunday Brunch 11:30AM - 2:30PM
except July & August. Dinner seven days.

Closed: Major Holidays

General Manager: Dominique Paulin, Public Relations: Georgette Farkas

Executive Chef: Gavin Kaysen, Pastry chef: Raphael Haasz

Maître d'Hôtel: John Winterman, *Wine Steward:* Emanuel Moosbrugger

Groups (max. group size): 10

Payment: Amex, Mastercard, Visa, Diners

Price: $65 and up per person

Ratings: 1 Michelin Star, Zagat: Food 27, Service 26

Reservations: Recommended, *Dress Code:* Casual chic-no tie required

Architecture: James Harb, *Interior Design:* Patrick Naggar, Nile Inc.

Notable features: Wine list with vintages from every continent with up
to 450 selections arranged by grape variety. Custom Designed China by
Bernardaud, Limoges, France

From top left to bottom:
• Peekytoe Crab Salad, Watermelon Radish, Cucumber Fennel, Saffron Clementine
  Vinaigrette
• Lemon-Chocolate Bar, Hazelnut Bavaroise, Puffed Rice, Perrier Lemon Sorbet
• Indian Spiced Lamb Duo, Crispy Samosa, Red Lentils, Cucumber and Radish Raita

Food Fears

Endless delight or nagging fear? For all that we would much rather reflect on regarding the pleasures that food affords, contemplating the glorious meals of yore, dreaming of those yet to come, the most intrepid eater among us hesitates.

We worry: "Will I make this food me, or will it take over my body?" We fear invasion because we fear losing our identity – the food may turn out to be stronger than we are. We no longer control our bodies. A Circe in the kitchen may turn us into swine as the goddess did the companions of Odysseus.

That we eat anything at all points to the importance of culinary trust. Even for the foods that we know, or think we know, we have to assume that cultivation or storage or transportation or preparation or additives will not trouble our tummies. We trust food encounters of the past to ensure pleasure in the present.

Allergy sufferers know full well that bodily integrity comes at the price of eternal vigilance. We don't leave home without an Epipen. We read labels compulsively and scrutinize menus, we interrogate waiters ("nuts and peanuts, yes, I know they're not the same but I'm allergic to both") and we justify inconsistencies ("pine nuts aren't nuts, and I love them"). Like all tastes, allergies also bring (some of) us together. The comaraderie of the afflicted grows every day ("You're allergic, too!"). In time we acquire a vigilante network on the lookout for our debility. A friend checks her supplies ("The new jar of jam is just for you, no peanut butter-laden knives have touched it"), a spouse puts the restaurant on notice ("We have an allergy at the table"), a restaurant tracks preferences ("Madame cannot have the chocolate cake").

And we trade narratives of epic encounters with the Enemy. ("Let me tell you about…"). We have vanquished it – or we wouldn't be here to tell the tale – but the battle cannot be won, only set aside for another time. So we taste, we eat. Our pleasure all the more intense because we have once again navigated Scylla and Charybdis; the tempting and the forbidden.

Priscilla Parkhurst Ferguson

Cappuccino after 11 a.m.

Travelers to foreign countries often find themselves confronted with surprising cultural conundrums. Some can be avoided by reading up on the country one is traveling to. Spanish travel guide Anaya, for example, warns Spanish travelers as follows with regard to dining customs in Holland: "Keep in mind that, while it is considered normal to dine at 10 or 11 p.m. in Spain, the Dutch customarily dine early in the evening, between the hours of 6 and 8 p.m."

However well prepared, one can still be caught by surprise by something very simple, such as knowing the proper time of day to drink a cappuccino, for example. To be sure, this custom varies radically even within the boundaries of a given country. In Northern Italy, one routinely orders cappuccino after lunch, whereas in Sicily, such a thing is simply not done.

While traveling in Sicily in the 1990s I mentioned the no-cappuccino-after-mid-morning rule to my traveling companion. He couldn't imagine it to be true; in fact, he thought I was pulling his leg. Not being one to let an opportunity pass me by, I asked if he would like to make a small wager on the matter. If he witnessed a single Sicilian, during the remainder of our trip, drinking a cappuccino after 11 in the morning, I would treat him to a Michelin three-star dinner, including cappuccino to round out the meal!

We traveled around the island for ten full days. Search though we might, we found not a single Sicilian sipping cappuccino after mid-morning had passed. But then, on the evening of our last day, as we relaxed at an outdoor café, our attention was drawn to a distinguished signore at the table next to us. His face was partly obscured by the pages of the "Corriere della Sera", but it was quite evident that as he skimmed the evening headlines, he was drinking a cappuccino. My friend burst into laughter and advised me to place our three-star reservations. The gentleman, who had apparently been following our conversation, lowered his newspaper and commented dryly: "I'm afraid I'll have to disappoint you. I am a mere tourist, a Dutchman like yourselves, but you should have been able to tell that by my cappuccino."

Maarten van der Jagt

Chanterelle
2 Harrison Street (at the corner of Hudson Street)

Chanterelle

Address: 2 Harrison Street, New York, NY 10013
(at the corner of Hudson Street in lower Manhattan)
Phone: (212) 966 6960, *Fax:* (212) 966 6143
Internet: www.chanterellenyc.com, *Email:* inq@chanterellenyc.com

Cuisine: French Cuisine with Global Influences

Chef and Co-Owners: David and Karen Waltuck

Business hours: Lunch 12:00PM – 2:30PM Thursday – Saturday,
Dinner every evening starting at 5:30PM (5:00PM Sunday)

General Manager: George Stinson, *Special Events:* Amy Ehrenreich

Pastry chef: Kate Zuckerman

Master Sommelier: Roger Dagorn
Fromager (Cheese): Adrian Murcia

Special Events including Private Dining and Catering Available

Payment: Amex, Mastercard, Visa, Diners, Discover

Price: $42 and up per person

Ratings: 2 Michelin Stars, Zagat: Food 27, Service 27, *NY Times: 3 stars*

Reservations: Recommended, *Dress Code:* Casual chic-no tie required

Interior Design: Bill Katz. Set in the 19th century Mercantile Exchange
Building in TriBeCa with carved cherry wood pilasters, custard colored
walls, ornate tin ceiling, and soaring floral arrangements.

Notable features: Artworks on menu covers by a wide range of
distinguished artists, photographers, musicians and writers among them
Roy Lichtenstein, Cy Twombly, Keith Haring, Francesco Clemente and
Cindy Sherman. All the covers are framed and exhibited in the anteroom
near the reception area.

From top left to bottom right:
• A Trio of Chilled Spring Soups
• Steamed Scallops and Foie Gras Dumplings with Mushroom Vinaigrette
• Seared Duck Breast with Hot & Sour Duck Jus & Duck Spring Rolls
• Rhubarb-Almond Tart with Tarragon Scented Crème Anglaise

Adventures in chocolate

Chocolate-wise, times are changing. New York City is something of a chocolate paradise. Specialty shops dot the cityscape – American chocolatiers Marie-Bell and Vosges give comfort in SoHo and the Upper East Side, along with French transplant François Payard; Jacques Torres started chocolateering in Brooklyn, moved to SoHo and now sustains the Upper West Side as well. Then there are the French exports, La Maison du Chocolat and the venerable Debauve et Gallais (founded in 1829) on and just off upper Madison Avenue. Add to these the Belgian and Swiss' more broadly marketed Lindt, Godiva, Leonidas, and it becomes clear that New Yorkers are in chocolate paradise.

But you don't need specialty shops for your chocolate fix. A pretty ordinary supermarket turns up an assortment of chocolates that Hershey in the good old days never dreamed of. For that matter, even Hershey's isn't the same. Its own up-market brands of dark chocolate are pushing the common milk chocolate bars off to the side, if not out of the display case.

A mere 20 years ago, chocolate talk didn't exist. Today, one can (pretentiously) invoke a Chocolate Discourse. Topics no one thought about and certainly didn't talk about, give rise to impassioned debates. Is Venezuela cacao superior to Mexican or is Brazil *the* source for cacao? A particularly striking element of Chocolate Talk that is certainly a sign of the times is the insistence on the personal, responsible link between grower and chocolatier.

Chocolate, we are told over and over again, is good not only for the consumer and the artisan, but for the environment and the producer. For the consumer, chocolate brings pleasure without end (there is always more chocolate to be had). We are exhorted to "Discover the secret world inside this box – a place of beauty, works of art, pieces of joy." Or choose antioxidant dark chocolate "to support lasting inner strength." Good chocolate these days is dark chocolate plus – high cacao content with luscious and unusual fillings or infused with new flavors. No longer a staple, chocolate takes us on a gastronomic adventure.

Today's chocolate is a "multi-cultural citizen of the world," the Paris Salon du Chocolat proclaims, and a good citizen at that. Fair trade practices ensure the well-being of developing countries rather than their exploitation. One chocolatier even brought along his (tall, dark and handsome) grower from Brazil for the New York Chocolate Show in 2007.

A veritable artisanal chocolate revolution has set chocoholics to endless debates. Beyond the creams, nuts and caramels of the ever-popular Whitman's Sampler (introduced in 1912!), we have arrived in the land of haut-chocolat. Chocolate turns up infused with everything from the familiar (vanilla, lavender), traditional (rose water, citrus) and the popular (peanut butter) to the historical (chili), the startling (wild Tuscan fennel pollen, sake) and the frankly improbable (horseradish and lemon zest, wasabi), not excluding the pretty much unknown (Aboriginal anise, myrtle). The chocolate revolution has even hit milk chocolate. With less sugar and more cacao, this mass-market confection bids fair to vanquish the disdain of the truest chocolate aficionado.

What about chocolate lovers in exile? Those who, by design or by duty, find themselves far from chocolate-strewn metropolitan streets? The Internet to the rescue! Once upon a time, small chocolate makers had largely local followings. Indeed, the setting was integral to the chocolate, and customers associated small-town confectioners with vacations or the neighborhood candy maker with childhood treats. Today's chocolatiers stress instead the creativity of the artist and the integrity of the product. Instead of a staple selection of recognizable chocolates, contemporary chocolatiers parade a continually renewed display of products to the virtual world. FedEx and UPS are vital links in the chocolate chain, which makes chocolate heaven but a few clicks away.

Priscilla Parkhurst Ferguson teaches cultural sociology at Columbia University and spends a lot of time thinking and writing about food. Besides studies of French literary culture and Paris in the 19th century, she has written numerous articles on food in its cultural settings as well as a book on French culinary culture, Accounting for taste: The Triumph of French Cuisine (2004, French translation for 2009). See www.sociology.columbia.edu/fac-bios/ferguson/faculty.html

Daniel
60 East 65th Street (Between Madison and Park Avenues)

Daniel

Address: 60 East 65th Street, New York, NY 10065
(Between Madison and Park Avenues)
Phone: (212) 288 0033, *Fax:* (212) 396 9014
Internet: www.danielnyc.com

Cuisine: French-American Cuisine inspired by the seasons

Chef-Owner: Daniel Boulud

Business hours: 5:45-11PM, closed Sunday

Executive Chef: Jean François Bruel, *Chef de Cuisine:* Eddy Leroux

General Manager: Pierre Siue *Private Dining Manager:* Ryan Buttner

Pastry chef: Dominique Ansel

Sommelier: Philippe Marchal, *Cheese Steward:* Pascal Vittu

Maître d'Hôtel: Maite Montenegro

Groups (max. group size): 8 in the Main Dining Room – or up to
90 guests in the Private Dining Room

Payment: Amex, Mastercard, Visa, Diners

Price: $105 for 3 course prix fixe menu; $175 for 6 course prix fixe menu

Ratings: 2 Michelin Stars, Zagat: Food 28, Service 28, NY Times: 4 stars

Reservations: Recommended, *Dress Code:* Jacket required

Interior Design: Adam D. Tihany

Notable features: elegant lounge and bar for pre-dinner cocktails or after
dinner aperitifs, private dining room for up to 90 guests

From top left to bottom right:
- Peekytoe Crab Salad with Avocado
  Boston Lettuce, Minted Yogurt-Cucumber Gazpacho
- Duo of Abalone: Slow Baked with Paprika, Cauliflower Purée,
  Tempura with Early Mesclun, Ibérico Ham
- Pennsylvania Squab: Leg and Foie Gras Pastilla with Young Radishes
  Broiled Breast with Vadouvan, Avocado Chutney
- Honey Mousse with Vanilla-Rhubarb Compote
  Sheep's Milk Yogurt Sorbet

Stuffed animals

Men's Vogue Spring 2006

Is foie gras the height of gastronomic pleasure or murder most fowl? Honk if you've been force-fed.

Your sweet scent is a lyre / On our palates. / Your harmony / Plays cymbals on our tongues / And runs through us / With a long shudder of pleasure. – Pablo Neruda on foie gras

Do you think it's all right to eat foie gras? That would be an easy question if foie gras were not one of the most delectable foods on Earth. If they passed a law banning broccoli, nobody would utter a peep, except for farmers whose livelihood depends on broccoli. Plus a few peeps from people whose inexplicable yearning for broccoli cannot be satisfied by brussels sprouts.

Foie means "liver"; gras means "fat." It's French. Foie gras is the fattened liver of a force-fed duck or goose. These days 80 percent of the world's foie gras comes from ducks. Their livers expand by eight to ten times during the final month of feeding. Animal-rights advocates, notably PETA and Farm Sanctuary, argue that force-feeding ducks is cruel and causes unacceptable suffering. The practice is illegal in Argentina, two-thirds of Austria, the Czech Republic, Denmark, Finland, Germany, Ireland, Israel (until recently a large producer of foie gras), Italy, Luxembourg, Norway, Poland, Sweden, Switzerland, the Netherlands, and the United Kingdom, most of which never produced foie gras in the first place. I've heard that Israeli farmers are thinking of moving their operations to the West Bank; most of their current workers now are Palestinians.

Foie gras is the new fur. Except that you can't eat fur. Foie gras is an incomparably delicious food, and there's no substitute, no such thing as faux gras. What does it taste like? Most writers use the word buttery, but if that were all, you could save lots of money and grief by eating butter. I'd like to take a stab at it, but I'd first have to eat lots more foie gras, and I can't do that until I decide whether it's ethically right. Maybe now is the time to decide. We can't put it off forever.

I had my first taste long ago, when I was 20 and on a trip to Europe with two old friends. We had saved up for a three-Michelin-star meal in Paris, at the restaurant Laserre. (In those days you could hold the bill to $15 if you were careful ordering wine.) My first course was a generous round of foie gras baked into a buttery brioche pastry encircled by a very light and savory version of sauce Périgueux – meat juices reduced with Madeira and flavored with finely minced black truffles. I ate more and more slowly so that it would never disappear. It taught me that there were gastronomic worlds I had never even imagined.

A whole, raw foie gras is naturally pink-beige and shiny and weighs about a pound and a half. It can be eaten hot – in crisp, dark-brown sautéed slices with creamy insides, the most popular form in restaurants these days; or braised until evenly tender throughout, then dramatically served whole at the table; or poached in its own fat or turned into a luxurious sausage, or pureed into a soup with chestnuts, or wrapped into dumplings or turnovers, or confected into an eggy custard, which is among my favorites. Then it is best accompanied by something acidic and fruity. When foie gras is served cold, it is often in a terrine – mildly flavored with cognac or liqueur and pinches of spice and salt, or not flavored at all, then pressed into a loaf pan and baked until the insides are barely hot (unless you follow USDA warnings), and finally cooled and allowed to develop its flavor for a day or two. (You can see a hundred ways of cooking foie gras in an excellent book, Foie Gras: A Passion, by Michael Ginor with Mitchell Davis and others.) People who don't know anything much about foie gras promiscuously call it pâté. Pâté de foie gras is something distinct, a mixture of ground foie gras and pork or veal or duck, baked en terrine and cooled. In France, pâté de foie gras must contain at least 50 percent foie gras, but it doesn't compare to pure, unalloyed foie gras, the genuine article.

Traditional force-feeding in the southwest of France, where foie gras is a historic specialty, is still done on some small farms by a member of the farmer's family, who inserts the tube end of a funnel filled with corn some inches down the duck's throat while massaging its neck. This aids the passage of food and checks that there is no corn left over from an earlier feeding. An auger revolving within the tube can also propel the corn. This method of feeding is known as gavage.

Many varieties of duck are migratory, and they instinctively overeat before the long voyage; birds have the remarkable ability to store excess nutrients as fat in their livers, which regularly double in size, but not much more than that without force-feeding. (As you may have noticed in the mirror this morning, mammals store fat all about their bodies and not in their livers, unless they are very sick.) The duck's anatomy also includes a crop, "a pouchlike enlargement of the esophagus... in which the food undergoes a partial preparation for digestion before passing on to the true stomach," according to the Oxford English Dictionary. Ducks don't chew – they have no teeth, and they have no gag reaction. A duck's crop can hold the excess corn it is fed, unless it is forced to swallow too much, in which case some of the corn gets forced into the bird's stomach or clogs its throat, a rare occurrence when ducks are fed by hand. The ducks are kept in an ample yard and crowd around the feeder when she appears. Near the end, when their fattened livers weigh a pound or more, the ducks may possibly have trouble walking.

This is about as benign as force-feeding gets. It accounts for less than 20 percent of French foie gras and an indeterminate amount of foie gras in America. If what I've described is too harsh for you, then you'll not be consuming much foie gras, until they've found a nicer way to fatten a duck's liver. To me, this is acceptable. Industrially produced foie gras is not.

If Jesus were alive today, would he eat foie gras? The New Testament offers no guidance. I've skimmed all four Gospels, and I have yet to find a scene in which Jesus is actually eating, except maybe the dinner in the house of the Pharisees, which was so totally tense that I doubt anybody ate much of anything. Nor is there even one verse about the humane treatment of animals. I went out and bought a popular book called What Would Jesus Eat, by Don Colbert, M.D. It was in the Christian Inspiration section of my local Barnes & Noble. There's not a word in it on the foie gras issue. There's nothing about animal cruelty. Or about what Jesus did, in actual point of fact, eat. But I'll bet he never ate pork or lobster, because Jesus was a Jewish person. Colbert guesses that Jesus mostly ate manna. My corner bodega is plumb out of manna.

Is it possible that Jesus actually did eat foie gras? It certainly is an ancient delicacy. The Egyptians force-fed geese, though their purpose was most likely to obtain nice fat geese for the table, not fat livers. The first people to value the liver in itself were, naturally, the Romans. In his Natural History, Pliny the Elder wrote, at about the time of Christ, "Our countrymen are wiser, who know the goose by the excellence of its liver. Stuffing the bird with food makes the liver grow to a great size, and also when it has been removed it is made larger by being soaked in milk sweetened with honey." The Romans employed Jewish slaves to force-feed their geese, and the Jewish aristocracy in Palestine emulated the Roman upper classes as their social models. Foie gras would have been just the thing.

Throughout the Dark and Middle Ages, it was the Jews who kept alive the art and science of fattening geese. By the year 1100, many Jews had migrated to France and northern Germany, and with them went the practice of force-feeding geese. As they were prohibited from eating lard and could no longer obtain the olive oil of the Mediterranean, their only cooking medium was poultry fat, and a force-fed goose was the most abundant source of schmaltz known to man or woman. But the great French-Jewish medieval scholar Rashi worried that the Jews would have to pay in the afterlife for the force-feeding they practiced. In those days, I've read, the geese were blinded and their webbed feet nailed to the floor.

By the time of the Renaissance, Jewish butchers were serving Christian lovers of fatted goose liver in Italy and northern Germany, and Strasbourg in Alsace became the world capital of foie gras. When Germans immigrated to the Midwestern United States in the nineteenth century, they brought with them the talent for force-feeding geese. Watertown, Wisconsin, was the center of the stuffed-goose industry, according to the Watertown Daily Times, which characterized it as an old German tradition; the force-feeding was accomplished with noodles. Until the 1970s, Watertown supplied German butcher shops in New York City and the storied restaurant Lüchow's, on Fourteenth Street. People believe that the later influx of relatively inexpensive semi-cooked French foie gras put the Midwest farmers out of business. But for all we know, the German-American housewives of Wisconsin still hasten to their poultry sheds under cover of night to stuff their geese. I guess this means that force-feeding geese is as American as SnackWell's or Kraft Singles.

So far, the animal-rights people have not succeeded in France, which is the largest producer and consumer in the world – 17,500 tons a year.

The foie gras industry there has created 130,000 jobs, direct and indirect, and in 2005, the national assembly declared foie gras a "cultural and gastronomic patrimony protected in France." In the United States, foie gras is produced on only three farms, two in New York State and one in Sonoma County, California. In late 2004, the California legislature passed a bill (S.B. 1520) banning the production or sale of foie gras, and Governor Schwarzenegger signed it into law. Although this was generally seen as a great victory for the anti-foie gras forces, it was in reality just a tiny triumph because the ban goes into effect in 2012, and until then the one producer in the state is shielded from civil lawsuits. The response of animal-rights groups was divided. Some were outraged, seeing the new law as a betrayal; others, for various reasons, preferred to claim it as a famous victory. California has seen episodes of vandalism and harassment against restaurants, private houses, and Sonoma Foie Gras, a small, largely artisanal farm. The animal-rights people seem to be as strongly convinced of their cause as anti-abortion protesters.

Early in 2005, a bill against the production of foie gras in New York State was posted on the legislative calendar. This could have been cataclysmic for foie gras lovers, as most of the foie gras in the United States comes from a company called Hudson Valley Foie Gras, in Ferndale, New York. Michael Ginor, its proprietor (and the coauthor of Foie Gras: A Passion), helped write the law himself, which included a ten-year grace period. Ginor tells me that he simply wanted the kind of certainty a businessman needs to make decisions, such as whether to put a new roof on a barn. Understanding that Ginor truly did not want the bill to pass, the Republicans in the state Senate killed it. No new bill appears to have been posted this year. Have I found the one reason to vote Republican?

In the abstract, the foie gras question is simple. All Americans fall into one of three categories: Some believe that exploitation of any animal, even milking a cow or taking honey from a hive, is immoral, impermissible. I don't fall into this small group and neither, probably, do you. At the opposite extreme are people who argue that man was created at, or evolved to, the top of the heap and can do whatever he wants with other species, even administer agonizing pain. I've been surprised to discover how many of my fellow humans make this claim. I'm not in that category either. If you are, then you'll happily continue to gorge on foie gras while the rest of us follow a middle way.

Most of us are not vegans or vegetarians. When we buy the flesh of a mammal, bird, or fish in a restaurant or food shop, we are an agent in the slaughter of another living thing. We are taking life. This is a serious act, not a casual one. But our purpose is not survival or even sustenance; most of us can live comfortably without eating meat. No, our goal is pleasure, pure sensory pleasure. We chew on the succulent muscle of a steer, crunch through the crackling skin of a pig or turkey, suck out the marrow from the shin of a calf. If we are willing to kill for our pleasure, shouldn't we also be willing to force-feed ducks for our pleasure? It all depends on how much pain and distress we cause.

Although they neglected to nominate me for sainthood in the last go-around, I do try to follow a few modest practices. I don't eat animals that were raised or slaughtered chemically or inhumanely, preferring animals that grew up in pastures and fields, were cared for individually and by hand, and were not given growth hormones or unnecessary antibiotics. I don't eat veal from anemic calves confined in the darkness of a crate that keeps their meat desirably pale. I haven't eaten supermarket pork for the past ten years, except at important Southern BBQ events. Or eggs laid by battery hens. Or chickens on growth hormones raised by the thousands on the floors of barns covered with several weeks of their own waste – except when they have been fried by an incontestable master. I don't eat meat that doesn't matter – crumbled onto a pizza or scattered over a slimy salad or cooked to cardboard grayness and wedged between two buns. Meat and fowl of the highest quality are extremely expensive, and so I can't afford a great quantity of them. This cuts down on the volume of slaughter for which I'm responsible, as does my attempt not to waste animal flesh. That is how I've made my peace with slaughter.

Animal-rights advocates are much more likely to be vegetarians, vegans even, than the rest of us. That's been my experience. They argue for humane husbandry and slaughter, but underneath it all they won't rest until we stop killing animals for food. Foie gras is an easy target. Luxurious and expensive, it is eaten by only a fraction of the populace, and for much of the rest it carries the stink of decadence and excess. In France, foie gras has long been a required part of Christmas dinner, so being against foie gras in America is deliciously, mouthwateringly anti-French.

In this country, the animal-rights people distribute documented, photographed examples of revolting scenes in the barns and feeding sheds. Foie gras producers argue that the number of injured, ill, or prematurely dead ducks and geese is less than in the average poultry operation. Most of these problems can be ameliorated by getting closer to the artisanal, hands-on methods of the French housewife in southwest France. In the United States, improving the conditions of tube feeding can be achieved through regulation instead of prohibition. After all, there are just three foie gras farms in the entire country – it's not a difficult activity to watch.

And so, at last, the question comes down to this: How much distress does the most careful sort of tube feeding cause to the duck? I know of only two medical or scientific attempts to answer this question. Neither of them has been cited by animal-rights advocates, who instead encourage us to anthropomorphize, to imagine how we would feel getting tube-fed and fattened. But this may be the wrong question. How would we like to be a duck under any circumstances? How would we feel having to paddle all day on cold New England rivers and among the sodden marshes? I wouldn't be able to take it. Think of all the bugs and crawling things. Isn't there a better way of gauging a duck's distress?

Maybe there is. I telephoned Daniel Guémené, Ph.D., a research director at INRA, the prestigious French Institute for Agricultural Research. Guémené is an extremely prolific author of papers published in French and English journals, places such as World's Poultry Science and British Poultry Science. One of Guémené's keen interests is in discovering and refining ways of knowing whether poultry, ducks in this case, are in pain. He began his work on force-feeding in 1995, and as far as he can tell, his group at INRA is still alone in scientifically assessing the effect of tube feeding.

His first experiments examined the concentration of corticosterone – a hormone closely associated with stress – in ducks' bloodstreams before and after feeding. He expected a sharp rise – but found none at all. Over the following years, Guémené's group also looked at other indications of distress – avoidance of the feeder, withdrawal, pain signals in the medulla – and found possibly some pain in the final days of feeding, probably caused by inflammation of the crop; minor signs of avoidance, but not aversion, among some ducks at feeding time; and an increase in panting. Ducks showed the most stress when they were physically handled in any way or moved to new cages. Mortality on foie gras farms appears to be lower than in standard poultry operations. Guémené's group confirmed that although a grossly fattened liver is not natural, it is not a sign of disease; after feeding is stopped and the liver shrinks, there is no necrosis – no liver cells have been killed.

The American Veterinary Medical Association (the largest and oldest veterinary organization in America) has also considered tube feeding. In 2004, a resolution opposing the practice was introduced in its House of Delegates and referred to a study committee, which over the following year analyzed the limited amount of peer-reviewed literature and visited at least one of the three American foie gras farms. In July 2005, delegates presented their arguments on both the original resolution and a compromise version, apparently approved by an animal-rights representative. One opponent of tube-feeding who had made the farm visit conceded that the birds were not in distress or pain, that, although obese, they could still walk, and that they were better cared for than most chickens raised for food. But he still concluded that this was "not a good use of these animals." When a vote was taken, both ban resolutions were overwhelmingly defeated. Some delegates were influenced by the argument that if the organization disapproved tube-feeding, who knew what might follow? Why, next year they might condemn the confinement of veal calves, or the batteries of small, mechanized cages in which egg-laying hens are kept for their entire adulthood. Not a bad idea.

Well, there it is. The scientific evidence is pretty much unanimous in not condemning foie gras, but the evidence is still limited. So, though it seems unnecessary to stop eating foie gras altogether, the data is not unambiguous enough to encourage unbridled gorging. For now, the most sensible policy is to eat just a little of this sublime and ancient delicacy. Which is what most of us are doing already.

Jeffrey Steingarten

Degustation Wine and Tasting Bar
239 East 5th Street (Between 2nd and 3rd Avenues)

Degustation Wine & Tasting Bar

Address: 239 East 5th Street, New York, NY 10003
(Between 2nd and 3rd Aves.)
Phone: (212) 979 1012

Cuisine: Modern Spanish

Owners: Jack and Grace Lamb

Business hours: 6:00PM - 11:00PM, Closed Sunday

General Manager: Jack Lamb, Executive Chef: Wesley Genovart

Wine Steward: Chloe Nathan

Groups (max. group size): 4

Private Dining: Yes

Payment: Amex, Mastercard, Visa, Diners

Price: $6 - 18 small plates, $50 5 course tasting
and $75 10 course tasting menu

Food Ratings: 1 Michelin Star, Zagat: Food 26, Service 21,
New York Times: 2 Stars

Reservations: Yes

Dress Code: Casual

Interior Design: Hiromi Tsuruta

From top left to bottom:
- Slowly Poached Egg, Jamon Serrano, Chorizo, Smoked Cheese and Rice Cracker Crusted Asparagus
- Griiled Octopus, Potato, Cippolini Onions and Celery Salas with a Piquillo Pepper Emulsion
- Grilled Quail, Trompette Mushrooms and Toasted Pine Nuts
- Olive Oil Poached Cod, Guanciale, English Peas and Mussels

Del Posto
85 10th Avenue (Between 15th and 16th Streets)

Del Posto

Address: 85 10th avenue, New York, NY 10011
(Between 15th and 16th Streets)
Phone: (212) 497 8090, *Fax:* (212) 672 0390
Internet: www.delposto.com

Cuisine: Italian - Cucina Classica

Owner: Mario Batali, Joe Bastianich, Lidia Bastianich

Business hours: Sunday 4:00PM - 10:30PM,
Monday, Tuesday 5:00PM - 11:30PM,
Wednesday - Friday 12:00 - 2:00PM, 5:30 - 11:30PM,
Saturday 4:00 - 11:30PM

General Manager: Alfredo Ruiz

Executive Chef: Mark Ladner

Pastry chef: Brooks Headley

Wine Steward: Wine Director - Morgan Rich

Groups (max. group size): 10

Private Dining: 4 private dining rooms, Toscana, Barabaresco, Barolo and
Gattinara. Barolo and Barbaresco can be combined to form Piemonte.
up to 200 reception

Payment: Amex, Mastercard, Visa, Diners,

Price: $150 and up per person

Ratings: 2 Michelin Stars, Zagat: Food 25, Service 24, New York Times: 3 star

Reservations: highly recommended, *Dress Code:* smart casual

Architecture: Glen Coben, *Interior Design*: Lisa Eaton

Additional features: Green Restaurant Certified

From top left to bottom right:
- Garganelli Verdi al Ragù Bolognese
- Horseradish Panna Cotta with Insalata d'Astice & Sclopit
- Pork Loin with Lucanica, Ceci Spezzatino & Garlic Mustard
- Butterscotch Semifreddo
  Tri-Star Strawberries, Crumbled Sbrisclona & Milk Jam

Talking 'tomato'

It's weird, isn't it, that people only go into detail when they are talking about wine. There is even a whole lexicon dedicated to the 'palette of flavor impressions.' The humble wine enthusiast hardly dares utter a word when wine fanatics begin to spout a lot of trendy terminology.

I have never heard anyone speak about a tomato as something that "hasn't yet reached full maturity," or that "has a closed, or dumb, period." This can only refer to the development of a wine as it matures in the bottle; it has nothing to do with tomatoes. But the point is this: why is there such an endless stream of 'talk' about wine, and so little about something so lovely as the taste of a tomato?

I recommend the following taste test: Wait for a warm, summer day and take a trip to the shore. In your cool-pack, next to the "crisp, fresh Riesling with robust overtones of a mineral terroir," pack a couple of different varieties of bite-sized tomatoes. Spread your towel out on a quiet stretch of beach, and lie down on your back. Relax, and pick up the first tomato. Place it into your mouth but do not bite into it. Note that the tomato gives a fairly closed feel in your mouth. Bite, and taste! At that moment, I guarantee, you are tasting tomato! "Well that makes sense," you say, "since I'm lying in the sun eating a tomato." But that isn't what I mean. No, perhaps for the first time in your life, you are tasting, not eating, concentrated tomato flavor! And why not? There is nothing to distract you. Fully relaxed, you will find more and more flavors in the taste of that first tomato. It is characterized by impressions of tarragon and celery, and sweet anise-like undertones that contrast with the acidity of the tomato. That acidic flavor carries hints of apple and lemon. Try to bear in mind the duration of the tomato's aftertaste. Some tomatoes are good for a full ten minutes of fun. Before you know it, you'll be talking tomato. But then, from that day forward, you'll also be able to taste them.

Maarten van der Jagt

The sense and nonsense of:

Decanting
Decanting is the act of transferring the contents a bottle of wine into a carafe. In this way, young wines with a "closed character" are allowed to "air", which in turn makes them more enjoyable. Mature wines are decanted in order to separate the wine from any sediment that may be present in the bottle, and this must be done very carefully. Too much air will age the wine too quickly. Young white wines and sparkling wines should never be decanted.

Chilling
During this process, ice is placed into an empty glass and swirled around until the outside of the glass frosts over. At this point, the ice is discarded and the wine is poured into the glass quickly. We use this technique for pouring grappa, eau de vie, marc and liqueur, and for refreshing a wine that has become too warm.

Vin chambré: bringing wine up to its ideal temperature
This technique involves slowly allowing a wine that has been stored in a wine cellar to come up to its ideal temperature. This is important for all wines. A wine that is too cold will remain "closed", that is, it will not impart its best flavors to the consumer. Rather, the acidic flavors will remain prominent and the sweet flavors will be banished. Red wine that has been allowed to become too warm may be characterized by a strong alcoholic flavor.

Tasting the wine
It is traditional for the host of a restaurant gathering to "taste" the wine before it is poured for the other guests. Everyone looks on expectantly, waiting to see whether the first sip will be followed by an approving nod. This is a nonsense practice that stems from the days when wine bottles were stopped with wax rather than cork. To prevent guests having to swallow bits of crumbled wax that might have fallen into the wine, the host would sample the wine first. Today, the most practical thing to do is to have a sommelier taste the wine, and this is exactly what happens in the better French restaurants.

Thérèse Boer

Dévi
8 East 18th Street, (Between Fifth Avenue and Broadway)

Dévi

Address: 8 East 18th Street, New York, NY 10003
(Between Fifth Avenue and Broadway)
Phone: (212) 691-1300, *Fax:* (212) 691-1695
Website: www.devinyc.com

Cuisine: Indian Home Cooking

Co-Chefs/Owners: Suvir Saran and Hemant Mathur

General Manager/Partner: Sandeep Solomon

Business hours: 12:00PM - 2:30PM, 5:30PM - 11:00PM,
Sun: 5:00PM - 10:00PM, No lunch Sat and Sun
Closed: (Vacation) Major Holidays

Executive Chef: Hemant Mathur, *Pastry chef:* Surbhi Sahni

Groups (max. group size): up to 75

Private Dining: Semi-private dining

Payment: Amex, MasterCard, Visa

Price: $45 and up per person

Food Ratings: One Michelin Star, Two Stars New York Times
Three stars New York Magazine

Reservations: Recommended

Interior Design: Larry Bogdanow

Additional features: Catering for private events and delivery for
special requests.

From top left to bottom right:
• Kararee Bhindi
  crispy tangy okra, tomatoes and red onions
• Coconut Shrimp Curry
  coconut rice
• Bombay Bhel Puri
  rice puffs, tamarind & mint chutney, tomatoes, potatoes and onions
• Mango Cheesecake
  rosewater-almond cookie crust, mango pate de fruit, mango crisp

15 East
15 East 15th Street (Between 5th and Union Square)

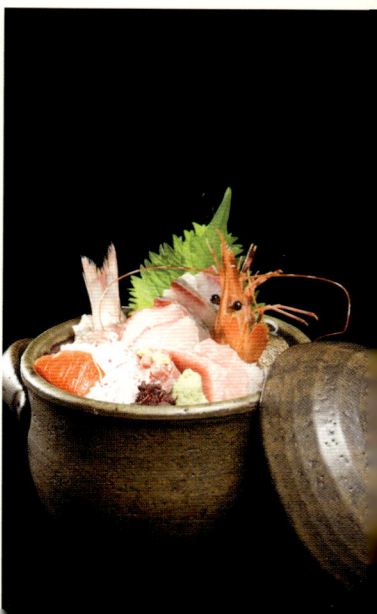

15 East

Address: 15 East 15th Street, New York, NY 10003
(Between 5th and Union Square)
Phone: (212) 647 0015
Internet: www.15eastrestaurant.com

Cuisine: Traditional Japanese with a modern flair

Owners: Jo-Ann Makovitzky and Marco Moreira

Business hours: 12:00PM - 2:00PM, 6:00PM - 10:30PM
No lunch Saturday, Closed Sunday

General Manager: Kim Wood

Executive Chef: Marco Moreira

Executive Sushi Chef: Masato Shimizu

Wine Steward: Aki Sonoda

Groups (max. group size): 45 buyout

Payment: Amex, Mastercard, Visa

Price: Prix-Fixe Lunch $29, Chef's Tasting 5 Courses $ 75

Ratings: Zagat: Food 26, Service 23

Reservations: recommended

Dress Code: Business Casual

Interior Design: Richard Bloch

Additional features: Prix Fixe Lunch

From top left to bottom:
- Tuna Flight
- Seared Bonito Salad with Mitsuba, japanese cucumber, miyoga and oroshi ponzu, shiso leaf flowers
- Slow poached octopus with natural sea salt
- Sashimi Omakase

The New Fulton Fish Market in New York

We were baffled for a moment as we made plans to visit the largest fish market in the world. Wasn't it located along the edge of Manhattan? Somewhere near the Brooklyn Bridge … on the water? We Googled it. It looked like the right spot, but it was called Fulton Street, not Fulton Market. Part of the old Fulton Fish Market had apparently been turned into a Health Center.
The street and the neighborhood were still there, but the Fish Market had been moved up to Hunts Point in the South Bronx in 2005. That's a shame; the South Bronx is quite a hike from lower Manhattan. It is also a shame for the many culinary early birds among the tourist population, because the boat-trip via Battery Park and the Circle Line to the Statue of Liberty and Ellis Island will no longer include a stop at the Fulton Market.

Until 2005, Fulton Fish Market was the early morning gathering spot of the New York restaurant crowd, whose representatives would start turning up around 5 a.m. to make their daily purchases. This was an example of New York folklore that was not to be missed by interested tourists.
But the move was deemed necessary because new legislation demanded higher standards for climate conditions. Also, after 180 years, the Fish Market had grown too large for its home, and plans were afoot to revitalize the area with new housing and retail establishments. The South Street Seaport and Fulton/East River were slated for demolition.

In Hunts Point, $86 million was invested in a modern, indoor fish market, where 37 businesses have staked their claim. It is the largest fish market in North America and after Tokio the largest fish market of the world; the merchandise that passes over its counters comes from the far corners of the globe, from the icy waters of Alaska to the tropical Caribbean.

We are given a guided tour by the chief of security, Mr. Klein, who comes in his surveillance vehicle to collect us at the gates of the Hunts Point Fish Market. Since 1988, the Fish Market has been held in trust by the U.S. Attorney's Office. All information pertaining to the market, such as types of fish offered for sale, their ports of origin and prices, are a matter of public record.

The long corridors house a cold, lively business. The hectic atmosphere of the merchants and their customers is infectious and it is wise to pay attention to where you are walking. Forklifts run all over, delivering the bushels and crates of purchased fish to the cooled delivery vans waiting in the immense parking lot outside.

Within 24 hours all these vans bring a variety of almost 100 kinds of fresh fish and seafood and about 80 varieties of frozen fish to restaurants and retailers, not only in New York, but all over America.

Tom Rietveld built an enterprise running shops and coffee counters in Dutch hospitals. After selling his business in 1988, he started Rietveld Creativity in Business in the Netherlands, and has received an Innovation Award FEM-PA. This summer his first book for children, "Unknown Fishes want to be Famous", is scheduled for release. Tom gives interviews and writes articles about people with culinary passion.

Eleven Madison Park
11 Madison Avenue (On the Northwest Corner of 24th and Madison Avenue)

Eleven Madison Park

Address: 11 Madison Avenue, New York, NY 10010
On the Northwest Corner of 24th and Madison Avenue
Phone: (212) 889 0905, *Fax:* (212) 889 0918
Internet: www.elevenmadisonpark.com

Cuisine: Market Driven French

Owner: Danny Meyer - Union Square Hospitality Group

Business hours: 11:30AM - 2:00PM, 5:30PM - 10:00PM

Sat no lunch, closed sunday and major holidays

General Manager: Will Guidara, *Executive Chef:* Daniel Humm

Wine Director: John Ragan

Groups (max. group size): 8

Private Dining: Yes, up to 50 guests seated and 100 standing cocktails.
646-747-2583

Payment: Amex, Mastercard, Visa, Diners

Price: $145 per person with wine, $100 per person without wine.

Ratings: Zagat: Food 26, Service 26, NY Times: 3 stars

Reservations: Recommended, 212-889-0905, www.opentable.com

Dress Code: Business Casual - No t-shirts, sneakers, or jeans.

Interior Design: Bentel and Bentel

Additional features: James Beard Awards: Rising Star Chef Nominee 04,
05, 07 - Chef Humm, Winner for Outstanding Wine Service - 2008:
Wine Director John Ragan

From top left to bottom right:
- Foie Gras, Terrine with Golden Pineapple and Pickled Pearl Onions
- Nova Scotia Lobster, Poached with Garden Peas, Oregon Morels and Mint
- Vacherin, Strawberries, Basil, and Black Pepper

Server: not just waiting tables

People sometimes ask me what it is that's so great about waiting tables: "isn't it just being subservient, and working your tail off precisely when everyone else is getting out of work?" With respect for everyone's right to his/her opinion, I have to say that people who think like this are far from the mark, especially when it comes to the way I think about our business.

When I first took charge of "the black brigade" at De Librije, I embarked o a process of profound professional growth. When I graduated from hotel school, I was qualified as a professional waitress. I was familiar with all of t trade techniques, but was still missing one essential component: experienc

Being a good server requires much more than simply waiting tables. As soon as a customer enters the restaurant, the server has to make a determination as to what that person is expecting. A couple in love won't want you hovering over them, but other customers may be eager to engage you in conversation.

Judging situations like these is what makes the profession lively and challenging; you have to be on your toes at all times, and you have to make use of your people skills.

I prefer the word "server" to "waiter" or "waitress". I like to emphasize th idea of "service." Together with my team, I make it my business to be of service to customers. And I have to say that I think we're on the right track

Thérèse Boer

Saffron, the world's most precious spice

When it comes to products that inspire fake substitutes, Saffron may be at the top of the heap. "Ground" saffron is extremely suspect, and should be kept at a wide radius, especially if one is looking for the savory aroma of the genuine article. Your chances of purchasing a genuine Louis Vuitton bag at a market stand in Bangkok are greater than those of purchasing real, ground saffron there.

This is not to say that one's chances are much better when it comes to the non-ground variant. Safflower blossoms are commonly used to make imitation saffron threads that may be sold as "poor man's saffron" or "bastard saffron." The safflower is a tall, thistly annual that blooms a saffron-yellow color and turns progressively red. Fine if you want to give your white t-shirt a splash of Brazilian color, but not so nice in the risotto. Be wary! Purchase your saffron from a reliable source, and expect to pay in the neighborhood of $2.50 per gram.

Genuine saffron threads are the dried stigmas of the saffron crocus flower (crocus sativus). The crocus is cultivated in Europe (Greece, Spain) but saffron fields flourish from Iran to China. The high price is explained by the huge number of stigmas required for one kilo of saffron; estimates of that number vary from 200,000 to 400,000 stigmas per kilo. The stigmas must be harvested carefully by hand, one at a time. Use saffron sparingly. Roast the saffron threads in your pan to release their flavor.

Maarten van der Jagt

Culinary journalist Maarten van der Jagt is author and editor-in-chief of various cookbooks for renowned chefs in the Netherlands and international culinary guidebooks and wine magazines. He is also a restaurant critic and coordinator of IENS, the online Dutch counterpart of Zagat's. He has been a food judge on many Dutch TV culinary programs, and has published manuals on espresso techniques.

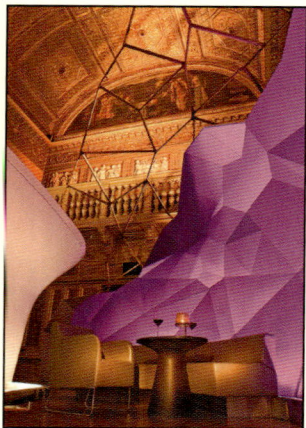

Gilt

455 Madison Avenue (Between 50th and 51st Streets)

Interior photography by Michael Kleinberg

Gilt

Address: 455 Madison Avenue (Between 50th and 51st Streets)
Phone: 212-891 8100, *Fax:* 212-891 8110
Internet: www.giltnewyork.com

Cuisine: Modern American

Business hours: Tuesday - Thursday 5:30PM to 10:00PM for dinner Friday and Saturday 5:30PM - 10:30PM Gilt Bar is open daily from 5:00PM to 1:00AM and the Bar Menu is offered daily from 5:00PM - 11:30PM

Closed: (Vacation) – Last two weeks in August

Restaurant Director: Christopher Day, *Executive Chef:* Christopher Lee

Pastry Chef: David Carmichael, *Service Director:* Brett Mendel

Director of Wines and Spirits: Jason Ferris

Groups (max. group size): 8 *Private Dining:* Up to 100 people sit down

Payment: Amex, Mastercard, Visa, Diners

Price: $85 for 3 course Prix-Fixe Menu. Tasting Menu $110 for 5 courses, and $140 for 7 courses. Bar menu prices from $12 - $30

Food Ratings: 1 Michelin Star (2007), Zagat, Food (2007) 25

Reservations: Highly recommended. Taken up to two months in advance over the phone, one month in advance on Open table

Dress Code: Jackets are preferred, ties optional. No sneakers or shorts.

Architecture: McKim, Mead & White, *Interior Design:* Patrick Jouin

Parking: Garage located on 50th st btw Mad & Park, wheelchair access, 2006 Food and Wine Magazine – Best New Chefs Winner/2005 James Beard Award Winner for Rising Star Chefs, 2007 Rising StarChef Award

From top left to bottom right:
- Shellfish & Seafood Paella: Saffron Rice, Sugar Snap Peas, Green Olive, Cherry Tomatoes, Orange Pernod Sauce
- Vadouvan Spice Crusted Veal Tenderloin
  Red Lentils, Cauliflower Florets, Date Puree, Broccoli, Sumac Yogurt Sauce
- Baby Mediterranean Octopus: Black Bean Puree, Potato Confit, Smoked Paprika, Chorizo Popcorn, Sauce Verde
- Seared Foie Gras
  Wild Strawberries, Sicilian Pistachio, Baby Basil, Key Lime Short Bread

How do great dishes acquire their names?

Inspired by Marie-Antoine Carème, the great early 19th century French chef who recorded and named all of the great French dishes, many chefs have dedicated their culinary creations to great statesmen and famous performers. Auguste Escoffier did just that when he created a special dessert for the Australian opera diva, Nelly Melba, at the Savoy in London in March, 1893. The dessert consisted of vanilla ice cream, two peach halves, and spun sugar wings, all made up in the shape of a swan, presented on a silver platter.

Escoffier spent most of his distinguished career in Britain, much to the chagrin of the French. In 1900, when he moved his operations to the new and larger Ritz-owned hotel, The Carlton, he reintroduced his "peach swan," newly enhanced by the addition of a lightly sweetened raspberry purée, and a new name: 'Pêche Melba.' Alas, this once exalted treat has now sunk to the status of an ordinary dessert consisting of vanilla ice cream, one tinned peach half, and bottled raspberry sauce.

Will Jansen

The wine list

A good restaurant must have a good house wine. That wine must be a quality product with a versatile flavor and character for broad appeal. I like keeping many different bottles open, so customers can order the proper wines to accompany the various courses of their meal without being required to purchase whole bottles.

Our customers enjoy sampling the quality wines we offer at reasonable prices. Our wine assortments, like our food menus, are designed to suit each changing season. In the summer, we stock crisp, fruity wines with not too many tannins, and perhaps a nice rosé. When autumn and the hunting season roll around, it is time for more robust, more intense wines.

I always keep the customer's wishes in mind as I advise them on choices of wine. It is great fun to help them enjoy the discoveries of the world of wine. This does not necessarily have to be expensive. Drinking wine should be a pleasurable experience, not one tainted by snobbery. We do have expensive wines in our cellars, and luckily, we have customers who order them. It is a little bit thrilling whenever we open and sample these special wines.

Every good glass of wine is like a breath of fresh air, a feast, a reason to celebrate. But more than that, it is an excellent complement to an excellent meal; a culinary feast.

Thérèse Boer

Gordon Ramsay at The London
151 West 54th Street (Between 6th and 7th Avenues)
Executive Chef Josh Emett shown on photos

Gordon Ramsay at The London

Address: 151 West 54th Street, New York, NY 10019
Between 6th and 7th Avenues
Phone: 212 468 8888, *Fax:* 212 698 8138
Internet: www.GordonRamsay.com

Cuisine: French
Chef-Owner: Gordon Ramsay
Business hours: 12:00PM - 2:30PM, 5:30 - 10:00PM
no lunch Sunday through Wednesday
Executive Chef: Josh Emett
Pastry chef: Ron Paprocki
Restaurant Director: Sean McAlinney
Chef Sommelier: Shawn Paul
Private Dining: Yes, 3 rooms seating up to 20, 60 and 80 and a chef's
table that seats 8
Payment: All major credit cards
Price: $45 for 3 course prix fixe lunch
$100 and up for dinner
Food Ratings: 2 Michelin Stars, Zagat 2008: 25 for Food, 25 for Service
and 24 for Décor "Top Newcomer"
Reservations: Recommended
Dress Code: Smart with a jacket preferred for gentlemen
Interior Design: David Collins
Additional features: Gordon Ramsay at The London is located within The
London NYC Hotel, part of LXR Luxury Resorts. A collection of renowned,
independent resorts and hotels located in preferred destinations
worldwide. All room service and meeting/banquet offerings are also
provided by Gordon Ramsay.

From top left to bottom right:
- Pressed Hudson Valley foie gras
  tapioca and calvados jelly, candied ginger, toasted sourdough
- Slow cooked sabelfish with butternut squash carpaccio, preserved
  cucumber and red wine vinaigrette
- Single-origin Venezuelan chocolate mousse, passion fruit,
  balsamic reduction and yogurt sorbet

Food and wine: teamwork

When composing a fixed menu, Jonnie starts with fish; he then moves on to meat, then cheese, and finally, to something sweet. Whatever he puts onto the plates, I round it out with the wines. I follow a couple of basic rules during this procedure: whites go before reds, young wines before mature ones, dry wines precede the sweet, and simple wines precede the more complex.

Some wines are extremely versatile, suited to accompany a broad diversity of dishes; these are gastronomic wines. Others are limited, best when served with a particular dish, at which time they show their invaluable merit. It is always exciting and surprising. We are always involved in an ongoing process to find the best food and wine combinations. We sample and re-sample, and we continue to discover surprising combinations.

We believe that a wine grower's distinctive style and a chef's individual approach are of the utmost importance to the success of any culinary endeavor. By discovering and creating unique combinations, we hope to provide customers with a delicious, meaningful dining experience that offers a wealth of varying flavors. When searching for the best possible combinations, we sometimes find ourselves pulling the rug out from under old, long-established beliefs to reveal surprising new realities.

Thérèse Boer

Tasting

When our son was still a toddler, he put everything in his mouth. It was gorgeous to see how he experienced the world via his tongue. The tongue can distinguish four basic taste groups: sweet, sour, bitter and salt. But we also taste with our eyes, our ears, our hands and our heart. Color gives a pre-indication of flavor. Before taking a single bite we know that a green apple will be crisper, harder and more sour than a reddish-yellow apple. Our ears help us as well. A raw carrot that doesn't give a satisfying "crack" when bitten into is accompanied by a cloying taste. And even the untrained ear knows that mineral water being poured into a glass will have a different sound than olive oil being poured into a pan. This is also true, in a subtler way, for wine.

When tasting wine, the most important organ is the nose. One first takes in the aroma of the bouquet, and after that, one takes one's first sip. This involves a sort of gargling technique that causes the wine to be mixed with air. The wine is held in the mouth until the entire tongue can process all of the flavors. But of course, one is not limited to just that first sip. The bottle is still full, and can be enjoyed down to the last aftertaste.

Thérèse Boer

Gotham Bar & Grill
12 East 12th Street (Between 5th Avenue and University Place)

Gotham Bar & Grill

Address: 12 East 12th Street, New York, NY 10003
(Between 5th Avenue and University Place)
Phone: (212) 620 4020, *Fax:* (212) 627 7810
Internet: www.gothambarandgrill.com

Cuisine: Modern American Cuisine

Chef-Owner: Alfred Portale, *General Manager:* Bret Csencsitz

Business hours: 12:00PM - 2:15PM No lunch Sat & Sun,
5:30PM - 10:00PM (Sat 5:00PM - 11:00PM, Sun 5:00PM - 10:00PM)

Chef de Cuisine: Adam Longworth, *Pastry chef:* Deborah Racicot

Maître d'Hôtel: Robin Gustafsson, *Wine Director:* Michael Neslon

Groups (max. group size): 9 to 20 Based on request and availability

Payment: Amex, Mastercard, Visa, Diners, *Price:* Average dinner is $85
and up per person, Lunch Prix-fixe 3 courses at $31

Food Ratings: 1 Michelin Star, Zagat: Food 27 Service 26, 3 Stars NYT

Reservations: 212-620-4020, *Dress Code:* Elegantly Casual

Architecture: James Bieber, *Interior Design:* James Bieber

Additional features: James Beard Most Outstanding restaurant in the
Nation, James Beard Best Chef, Alfred Portale, 3 Star Crains Business,
Top 100 restaurant NY Magazine, Time Out Magazine's 2008 readers
selection Best Perennial Restaurant, 20 Years and Counting.
Opening 2008 Gotham Steak in Miami and in 2009 Gotham Bar&Grill
in Las Vegas

From top left to bottom right:
- Crisp Soft Shell Crab: fingerling potatoes, haricots verts, red onion and
  chipotle, white wine lime emulsion
- Black Bass Ceviche Verde: honeydew melon, avocado, cucumber and radish
  jalapeño-lime emulsion
- Roasted Maine Lobster: jasmine rice, napa cabbage
  and honshimeji mushrooms coconut lime lobster reduction
- Grilled Octopus: fingerling potatoes, grilled leeks and caperberries
  aged red wine vinaigrette

Crustaceans, shellfish and wine

Lobster and langoustine require elegant wines, as does shrimp. In order to avoid any metallic flavor reactions that may occur when these seafoods are accompanied by acidic wines such as Pouilly Fumé or Sancerre, I like to recommend a spicy Alsatian Pinot Gris or a buttery Burgundy Chardonnay.

At De Librije, we recommend a white Albarino from Rias Baixas, Spain, to accompany our crushed raw langoustines. This is a very fruity, slightly sweet wine. Other good choices include a fino or Manzanilla sherry, a Vino Santo from Italy or an Arbois from the French department of Jura.

When the menu choice is sautéed langoustines, we recommend a French Chardonnay such as Domaine de Clovallon from Languedoc or the broad, complex Soave Classico Superiore from Inama. When we serve deep-fried langoustines with orange-prawn crackers, we recommend the Byron Pinot Noir, a surprising red California wine with an elegant woody aroma.

We serve a lot of scallops, mussels and oysters in season. Scallops acquire a lovely, sweet flavor when pan-fried that combines well with a Chardonnay, Pinot Gris, Maccabeo or Sauvignon Blanc from New Zealand. When the scallops are grilled, try a lightly chilled St. Amour (Beaujolais) or a red Sancerre as accompaniment. We cook up the first mussels of the season in an enormous pan. They are served up with a battery of crusty baguettes and remoulade, or garlic sauce. We like to have an ice-cold glass of beer with this meal, or perhaps a nice, chilled rosé from Tavel or Lirac.

Thérèse Boer

Cheese and wine

Much can be said about the many cheeses available today, as well as about the wines that accompany them. Port wines and the last swallows of red that remain into the cheese course notwithstanding, there are often better combinations.

Rich, flavorful goat cheeses with a dry structure go well with a stark white wine. I prefer a Sauvignon Blanc, especially when the goat cheese is young. More aged, stronger goat cheeses are better served with a Vouvray.

The sweeter wines go well, in general, with all manner of blue cheese. Roquefort, Fourme d'Ambert, Stilton and Bleu de Bresse cry out for a Sauternes. If that is reaching too high for you, choose a botrytis-affected wine that has a similar character, such as a Late Harvest Sémillon from Chili or a Botrytis Chardonnay from Australia.

With cheeses such as Munster, Epoisses and L'Armi du Chambertin, the best choices are Gewürztraminer, Riesling Auslese, Cream Sherry and Madeira, as these wines have enough body to balance the flavors of such cheeses.

Those last swallows of red wine, by the way, are an excellent accompaniment to Dutch cheeses, such as Gouda. A young Gouda also pairs up well with a nice Tawny or Vintage Porto. Old Dutch cheeses such as Reypenaer Grand Cru are stark in character, and go well with a full-bodied wine or a very old Porto.

Thérèse Boer

Gramercy Tavern
42 East 20th Street (Between Park Avenue South and Broadway)

Gramercy Tavern

Address: 42 East 20th Street, New York, NY 10003
(Between Park Avenue South and Broadway)
Phone: (212) 477 1025
Internet: www.gramercytavern.com

Cuisine: Refined, Seasonal American Cuisine

Owners: Danny Meyer

Business hours Main Dining Room: 12:00PM - 2:00PM,
5:30PM - 10:00PM, Fri - Sun 5:30PM - 11:00PM
No lunch Sat and Sun.

Business hours Tavern: Sun - Thu 12:00PM - 11:00PM,
Fri - Sat 12:00PM - 12:00AM

General Manager: Kevin Mahan

Chef: Michael Anthony, *Sous Chef:* Nick Anderer

Pastry chef: Nancy Olson

Beverage Director: Juliette Pope

Groups (max group size): 8

Private dining: Seats up to 22 guests for lunch or dinner

Payment: All major credit cards

Price: Main Dining Room: Lunch: $50, Dinner: $82 Prix Fixe
Tavern: Lunch: $45, Dinner: $45

Ratings: 1 Michelin Star, Zagat: Food 27, Service 27 and ranked NY's #2
Most Popular Restaurant, New York Times – three star review

Reservations: Recommended

From top left to bottom right:
- Warm Salad of Vegetables and Farro
- Sirloin & Short Rib Ravioli with Tuscan Bean Purée, Brussels Sprouts
  and Black Olives
- Smoked Trout with Sunchoke Purée and Pickled Onion Vinaigrette
- White Chocolate Macadamia Brittle Mousse with Rhubarb Sorbet

Sex and the City

Remember the *Sex and the City* episode where Carrie, dressed in couture and her tuxedo-clad Russian boyfriend, trade the opera for Big Macs at McDonalds? While fiction, this scene speaks volumes about what dining in New York City is about: there are no rules. You can wear a tux to the local diner or jeans to a three-star restaurant like Gotham Bar & Grill. Anything goes and there is something for everyone at any given moment.

In a city where real estate is at a premium, much of life in takes place in the public space of restaurants. From birthdays and marriage proposals, to divorce decrees, it has happened in a restaurant. My husband Charles and I were married at Wild Blue at Windows on the World and we celebrated our son Griffon's first birthday at Beacon. Now, it's true we are in the restaurant business and I married into an important restaurant family, but it's par for the course in New York, no matter your profession or family history.

Because so much of life in New York happens in restaurants, as a result they serve as memory points. I can return to a restaurant I've been to once and it instantly brings me back to another time, a *moment*. Take Sammy's Romanian on Chrystie Street. I've been there once or twice, maybe 10 years ago? Yet I know that the next time, be it tomorrow or 15 years from now, that I descend the stairs and take my first bite of schmaltz, I will be transported back to that exact moment when I first was there.

People always ask me, "What makes a great restaurant?" And I have to say there is no formula. It's more than good food and service. It's an intangible that I can barely describe. But when a restaurant has it, I *feel* it as soon as I walk in the door, and immediately know I want to come back, before one bite of food or sip of wine. Call it feng shui… magic?

As someone who advises restaurants for a living, one of my biggest pet peeves is when the chef makes the experience more about him or her than about the customer. We are guests in their "homes" and when I am made to feel as if a chef is doing me a favor by serving me, it is inevitably my last visit. This is the *hospitality* business, a sentiment which is sometimes lost.

It's impossible to pick a favorite restaurant; instead I have choices for different occasions. I could go to BLT Steak, Cookshop, Gramercy Tavern's front room or Bar Americain every night and never get tired. Why? Because they are full of that great energy I described earlier – the magic. And there is always something on their menus that I crave.

I am enamored with Michael Psilakis' Modern Greek cuisine at Anthos and am intrigued by the new wave of Italian restaurants in the city. I love Andrew Carmellini's food and can't wait to see what he does next. Alto is exciting; I love how there is this interesting dichotomy between the dining room, which is elegant and the food with its serious "yum" factor. Convivio which recently opened in Tudor City taps into everything I love about Italian food and way of life. Where else can one sit in an elegant room and pass bowls of pasta around as if you're in a downtown trattoria?

Morbid, maybe, but I often quip about the fact that I think I'll die in a restaurant. But considering my choices, I'll die happy.

Jennifer Baum is the President of Bullfrog & Baum, a full-service public relations, consulting and marketing firm that specializes in the hospitality and lifestyle industries. A graduate of Union College who also earned an MBA from New York University, Jennifer has been featured and/or quoted in The New York Times, The New York Post, and PR Week among other outlets.

Il Mulino
86 West 3rd Street (Between Sullivan and Thompson Streets)

All photographs courtesy of Il Mulino

Il Mulino

Address: 86 West 3rd Street, New York, NY 10012
(Between Sullivan and Thompson Streets)
Phone: (212) 673 3783
Internet: www.ilmulino.com

Cuisine: Classic Italian

Executive-Chef: Michael Mazza

Business hours: Open Weekdays 12:00PM - 2:30PM, 5:00 PM - 11:00PM

Closed: (Vacation) July

General Manager: Mike Grecco

Groups (max. group size): 10

Private Dining: Yes

Payment: Amex, Mastercard, Visa, Diners

Price: $100 and up per person

Ratings: Zagat: Food 27, Service 24

Reservations: Yes

Dress Code: Business Casual

Architecture: The Old World Italian Classical interior of Il Mulino is dark, filled with fresh flowers and beautiful accessories. There is a comfortable bar area, accompanied by a handsomely dressed tuxedo staff. There are two seating levels and a private room in the back.

**We are in the midst of opening three new locations: Atlanta, Aspen and Atlantic City!

From top left to bottom right:
• Pappardelle with Tomato Basil Sauce
• Tiramisu
• Veal Chop with Sage
All photographs courtesy of Il Mulino

The Emotion of Eating

If a company writes about "getting involved in the emotion of eating" and wants to "inspire the taste buds", you know they are passionate. If their products are referred to as "a collection" and the product line is marketed as "Architecture Aromatique", you know you are in for an exceptional experience. We are talking about micro-vegetables, a very small but very powerful ingredient in haute cuisine.

Micro-vegetables are young shoots of aromatic herbs or even seedlings of exotic trees. The seeds are from ancient varieties from all over the world. They have been researched extensively and are selected primarily for their surprising flavor. They have caused the culinary world to rethink the idea of garnish.

Cress is another name for micro-vegetables. There are cresses for every culinary need, whether you are looking for taste, smell, feeling or presentation. Pick the Tahoon Cress if you want a real earthy flavor. Try the Borage Cress for a fresh cucumber sensation. If you are looking for an unusual decorative element you have to see the Affila Cress with the beautiful curly extensions. There is the Shiso Purple with the stunning color and the Shiso Green, traditionally used with sushi and sashimi. Other notable cress varieties are Mustard Cress and Sakura Cress, each with their own distinct individual taste. The products are packed in patented, stackable cress boxes. The windowed covers make each box look like a mini greenhouse. All products are delivered to the kitchen alive and will keep growing to ensure freshness. They will be hand-picked by the chef and bursting with flavor when served.

Sechuan Buttons are one of the most remarkable products in the whole collection. They are very unique "flavor-makers", creating a totally new experience for those who first try it. Start by taking a tiny bite of kernels from this yellow flower button in your mouth. The initial lemon flavor is soon followed by an electric feeling (like licking a nine-volt battery). You'll feel a tingling on your tongue as the sensation moves through your mouth, almost like an anesthetic.

With products like these, who wouldn't get involved in the emotion of eating?

www.koppertcress.com

Photo: Nicolas Mazard

Jean Georges
1 Central Park West (at 59th Street)

Jean Georges

Address: 1 Central Park West, New York, NY 10023
(at 59th Street)
Phone: (212) 299-3900, *Fax:* (212) 299-3914
Internet: www.jean-georges.com

Cuisine: French

Chef-Owner: Jean-Georges Vongerichten

Business hours Jean Georges: 12.00PM - 2:30PM, 5:30PM - 11.00PM
Closed Sun, Sat no lunch
Business hours Nougatine: 7:00AM - 11:00AM, (Breakfast)
Sat - Sun 8:00AM - 11:00AM (Brunch)
12:00PM - 3:00PM, 5:30PM - 11:00PM, Sun 5:30PM - 10:00PM

General Manager: Philippe Vongerichten

Executive Chef: Mark Lapico, *Pastry chef:* Johnny Luzzini

Wine Steward: Hristo Zisovski

Groups (max. group size): 6, *Private Dining:* Yes

Payment: Amex, Mastercard, Visa, Diners, Carte Blanche

Price: $150 And up per person

Food Ratings: 3 Michelin Stars, Zagat Food: 26, Service 26,
4 Stars New York Times

Reservations: Recommended

Dress Code: Main dining room: Jackets required, no jeans or sneakers
Nougatine: Business casual

Interior design: Main Dining Room: Thomas Jull-Hansen,
Nougatine: Adam Tihany

From top left to bottom right:
- Egg Toast, Caviar and Dill
- Caramelized Akaushi Striploin, Sugar Snaps, Jalapeno & Parmesan
- Bluefin Tuna Ribbons, Avocado, Spicy Radish, Ginger Marinade
- Goat Cheese Gnocchi, Caramelized Baby Artichokes, Lemon and Olive Oil

Details are not just details

What makes a dinner a memorable experience? Are food and wine more important than the service; or has the design of the room a bigger impact on the overall experience?

It's possible these four main ingredients play an equally important role in a professional restaurant operation, but whether a restaurant is successful depends very much on the way the countless details involved in running a good restaurant are carried out.

Can the quality and creativity of all that has been developed by chef, maitre d', sommelier and designer be delivered without fail for each guest, day in day out? It's a tough challenge, since it is the sum of all these details that make up the final image of the restaurant. Like Charles Eames said, "Details are not just details – they make the product."

So how do top dining restaurants in New York City deal with delivering these details?

First impressions
There is no special secret to this one; what better way to make guests feel at ease and welcome than to receive them warmly with a smile?

The receptionist will have studied the arrival list and will already be familiar with the names of the guests and tables that have been allocated. Even first-time guests should have a sense of being recognized and expected at reception. The receptionist leads the guest with an open-hand gesture to the table where members of the service assist with seating.

The chairs cleverly facilitate seating by having a top part that swivels, allowing guests to get in and out from the table very comfortably. Ladies' bags can be placed on the little pull-out shelf on the chair. In case the dining room is a bit too chilly for an elegantly dressed lady, the restaurant may offer a cashmere shawl, matching the color of her dress.

The creaseless, hand-ironed Italian linen tablecloth feels smooth and rich, and the Limoges porcelain, Austrian glassware and Parisian silverware tell guests they have landed in a place where attention to detail matters. All is spotless and neatly arranged. Each place-setting is meticulously checked before service by physically sitting in each chair and observing the table-setting from the guest's perspective. Each little flaw is detected and corrected, ensuring a perfect setting for the start of the meal.

The table is uncluttered and, aside from the show plate and side plate, only one glass and small fork is to be seen. As no menu choices have been made at this stage, there is little point in having more on the table. For each course, the proper silver- and glassware will be brought.

Information about each reservation, such as the occasion, possible allergies, number of previous visits, is passed on to the waiters, sometimes in the form of a small card, or "soignee". This information can be crucial to the success of the evening.

The Food & Wine experience
Soon after being seated, the welcoming gestures of the kitchen arrive in the form of picture-perfect cold and warm amuses.

After ordering, guests are presented with a fine, flavorful selection of homemade breads. Much is expected from the synergy among ingredients, cooking techniques and presentation, as well as the creativity of the chef in question. Celebrity chefs and wine gurus have risen to stardom level and go out of their way to deliver excitement on the plates and in the glasses.

In terms of the menus themselves, some chefs change theirs every day, foregoing signature dishes, while others like to feature their specialties over a long period of time, encouraged by guests who keep demanding them.

New York, being a truly multi-ethnic city, can offer practically all the ingredients and cooking techniques of the world in its melting-pot streets. Top-notch restaurants offer several world cuisines, ranging from French, Italian, Austrian and Greek, to American, Indian and Japanese. Most of them have their own, contemporary interpretation of their original cuisine, combining old and new ingredients and cooking techniques.

A good way to really experience the flavor of the cuisine and the style of the chef is to opt for the tasting menu, which usually consists of five or six smaller courses (and often include a great vegetarian option these days).

One of the nice things about a top restaurant is that the kitchen brigade is very experienced and can fulfill special requests effortlessly, an attitude that can also be expected of the service team.

The sommelier will approach the table knowing which food has been selected. Matching wine with food has been and always will be a topic of much discussion. Some swear by pairing the entire menu with different tasting measures of wine; others much prefer to order a bottle of wine they like best.

Serving wines by the glass to match the creations of the chef has two advantages: difficult food and wine combinations can be avoided; and the wine consumption tends to be more moderate. Another idea is to serve less than a whole bottle but more than a glass by offering decanters in different sizes.

Cellars and their main wine lists have become very extensive indeed to accommodate the ever-increasing numbers of wine enthusiasts who appreciate selecting the precise year and winery he or she is seeking. Some restaurants offer two lists: a shorter one with several good wines (more practical for the less-seasoned diners), and a comprehensive one. When an expensive bottle of wine is sold, it may well be the wine that dictates the food and the chef is asked to create a menu around this special wine.

New restaurant concepts give wine full exposure with wine rooms, wine glass cabinets and wine stations. Specially designed decanters add drama to the ritual of drinking wine. Some of the menus go so far as to shun food ingredients that are simply too difficult to match with wine.

Fine dining service
Although the kitchen and service staff are often under considerable pressure when the dining room is busy, it is important never to allow any of this anxiety to transfer to the guests. Staff should always remain calm

and composed. The service brigade should employ a swift, assured pace; no one should look or act hurried and there is no running of any kind. When approaching a table, guests should not have the feeling that they are be charged at, but approached with elegance and style.

When the pressure is on, service-staff need to rely blindly on things to be in place, ready to use. Polished silverware, glasses, ironed napkins, clean decanters, pristine menus, etc., are the "mise en place". When this equipment is stored in the service stations close to tables, the service brigade can focus on the guests instead of worrying about finding equipment.

To ensure great service, the staff needs to be alert. A thorough awareness of the process, a preternatural anticipation by the servers and smooth coordination with the kitchen is essential. Asking the kitchen to prepare the next course as plates have been removed, placing the silverware on the table, and decanting and serving the wine before the next course arrives are all procedures that must be perfected to achieve a flawless routine of the service basics.

Keen observation and a trained eye for what comes next is second nature to a good service professional. Constantly scanning the tables, observing the facial expressions of the guests allows service staff to accurately anticipate the next course of action. For example, even though plates seem empty, the table cannot be cleared if guests are still enjoying their last bite.

Service staff members need to keep an eye out for each other as well as for the guests. Table-service is a team effort; colleagues need a nod at the right moment to serve or clear the plates. Serving or clearing the tables with more than one person adds richness to a guest's experience, especially if this is done swiftly and elegantly. No one should ever have to flag the service staff for attention, just as they should not have to get out of the staff's way or get the door themselves. A good restaurant anticipates its guests' needs and responds immediately.

How guests are addressed is another important aspect of service. Well-spoken staff members who have a pleasing tone and confident air are essential to a top dining room. They should be very well-informed about the restaurant and its offerings, but just as importantly, they should adopt a "never say 'no'" attitude, always working towards the goal of a successful evening for their customers. The old adage "treat others the way you would want to treated" is heard often in the industry and is probably the simplest and most effective way of getting the point across.

As the evening progresses, the first tables start to leave and be reset. The arrival of new guests is smooth and barely disrupts the dining room. Restaurants in the Big Apple have two seatings an evening, the first roughly at 5:30pm and the second at 8:30pm or so. The pace can seem a bit hurried to slow diners, but it's in keeping with New York's natural rhythm.

Also in keeping with New York's natural tendencies is the reservation. No restaurant likes an empty table, and that is especially true of a top restaurant in New York. Guests who have made a reservation are contacted one or two days in advance to confirm, which is important for business, but equally important for the atmosphere, as dining in a full restaurant gives that electric feeling of being part of a crowd that enjoys a good, and perhaps exceptional, thing together.

Expectations are high in top restaurants. The first thing the restaurant wants to ensure is the delivery of the quality of food, wine and service for which they have come to be known. But it is the extra attention that brings the "wow" factor in a dining experience. The extra course that was not foreseen, the extra taste of wine to compare against what has been selected, cut marshmallows from a large jar at the table, freshly baked small Madeleines with espresso, a small attention by the chef at the end of the meal, perhaps a signed menu. These are the details that will stick in guests' minds.

The right ambiance
The star designer and celebrity chef have teamed up to create some stunning dining rooms around the city. Signature designs appealing to the other three senses have become part of the attraction for diners.

Obviously, seating is one of the first items to consider when designing a restaurant. The best restaurants offer very comfortable seats with pleasant views. They should also be free from draft and annoying sounds. However good the restaurant may be, if guests are not comfortable with the seat they were given, they will not enjoy the evening.

It is fashionable for production areas such as the kitchen, bar and wine cellar to be integrated into the design, often becoming the architectural focal points. The openness of these layouts also improves the communication between kitchen, bar and service staff. The shorter the distance from kitchen to dining room, the quicker the service.

Now part of the showcase, some spectacular wine cabinets and wine rooms have been designed, adding to the allure of a restaurant's atmosphere.

Although they might not notice all the many details that have been imagined and finetuned for their dining pleasure, people are intuitively aware when the food, wine, service and interior design blend in harmonious accord. The success of each element should feed into the others, creating an efficient, yet captivating restaurant that not only satisfies, but elevates its guests on all levels.

Ronald Huiskamp
ronaldhuiskamp@hospitalityconcepts.eu

Ronald Huiskamp is a regular columnist for Reed Business Publications and has over 20 years of experience in the hospitality business with a focus on restaurant operations. He published "Great Restaurant Concepts", with photography by Jan Bartelsman, in 2001. Ronald is an international guest speaker on conceptual thinking in the hospitality industry.

Jewel Bako
239 East 5th Street (Between 2nd and 3rd Avenues)

Jewel Bako

Address: 239 East 5th Street, New York, NY 10003
(Between 2nd and 3rd Aves.)
Phone: (212) 979 1012

Cuisine: Japanese

Owner: Jack Lamb

Business hours: 6:00PM to 11:00PM, closed Sunday

Chef: Yoshihiko Kousaka

Wine Steward: Jack Lamb

Groups (max. group size): 12, *Private Dining:* Yes

Payment: All Major Credit Cards

Price: $25 And up per person

Food Ratings: 1 Michelin Star, Zagat Food: 25, Service: 25,
1 Star New York Times

Reservations: accepted, *Dress Code:* Casual

Interior Design: Hiromi Tsuruta

From top left to bottom right:
- Usuzukuri
  Live Fluke
- Sashimi Omakase
  Tuna, Yellowtail, Amberjack Red Snapper, Bass, King Samon Squid, Scallop,
  JP, Chutoro and Sweet Shrimp
- Uni Brulee
  Sea Urchin and Big Fin Reef Squid
- Sushi Omakase
  Ohtoro, Tuna, Stripjack, Ocean Trout, Golden Eye Snapper, JP, Barracuda,
  Chopped Jack Mackerel, Live Octopus, White Shrimp, Sea Eel, Sable Fish

Jojo
160 East 64th Street (Between Lexington and 3rd Avenues)

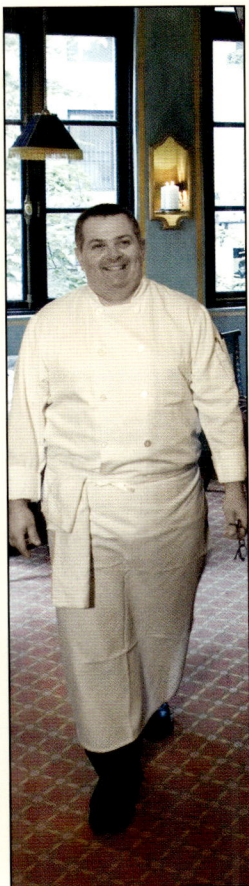

Jojo

Address: 160 East 64th Street
(Between Lexington and 3rd Avenues)
Phone: (212) 223-5656, *Fax:* (212) 755-9038
Internet: www.jean-georges.com

Cuisine: French Contemporary

Chef-Owner: Jean-Georges Vongerichten

Business hours: Mon-Thurs 12:00PM - 2:30PM; 5:30PM - 10:30PM

Fri-Sat 12:00PM - 2:30PM; 5:30PM - 11:00PM

Sun 12:00PM - 2:30PM; 5:30PM - 10:00PM

General Manager: Jamie Unwin

Executive Chef: Ron Gallo

Pastry chef: Eric Hubert

Maître d'Hôtel: Trisha Hitko

Groups (max. group size): 10

Private Dining: Yes

Payment: Amex, Mastercard, Visa, Diners

Price: $60 And up per person

Food Ratings: 1 Michelin Star, 3 Stars New York Times

Reservations: Recommended

Dress Code: Casual

Interior Design: Christophe Tollemer-based in St Tropez, France

From top left to bottom right:
• Goat cheese wax bean and cherry tomato salad
• Lobster roasted with new garlic, fresh corn and fingerling potatoes
• Cod roasted with marinated vegetables in an aromatic sauce
• Passion Pavlova whipped cream and passion seeds

Kuruma Zushi
7 East 47th Street, 2nd floor (between 5th and Madison Avenues)

Kuruma Zushi

Address: 7 East 47th Street, 2nd Floor, New York, NY 10017
(Between 5th and Madison Avenues)
Phone: (212) 317 2802, *Fax:* (212) 317 2803

Cuisine: Japanese

Chef-Owner: Toshihiro Vezu

Business hours: 11:30AM - 2:00PM, 5:30PM - 10:00PM, closed Sunday
Closed on National Holidays

General Manager: Hideki Takao

Groups (max. group size): 10

Private dining: 4-8 seats

Payment: Amex, Mastercard, Visa, JCB

Price: $50-$500

Ratings: 1 Michelin Star, Zagat: Food 28, Service 21

Reservations: recommended

Dress Code: Casual

Additional features: Fresh fish from Japan prepared daily

From top left to bottom:
- Russian King Crab (Body) Marinated
  Russian King Crab with Special Vinegar Sauce
- Sashimi
  Very Fatty Tuna, Fluke, Yellowtail, Kampachi, Kinmedai
- Sushi
  Very Fatty Tuna, Tuna Rolls, Kinmedai, Fluke, Kampachi, Shima, Aji,
  Salmon Egg, Smelt Egg
- Toro Caviar
  Very Fatty Tuna Tartare with Russian Osetra

L' Atelier de Joel Robuchon
57 East 57th Street (Between Park and Madison Avenues)
Shown in photo: Executive Chef Yosuke Suga

L' Atelier de Joel Robuchon

Address: 57 East 57th Street, New York, NY 100022
(Between Park and Madison Avenues)
Phone: (212) 350 6658, *Fax:* (212) 758 5711
Internet: www.fourseasons.com

Cuisine: Luxuriant and yet uncomplicated French cuisine

Owner: Ty Warner, *Founding Chef:* Joel Robuchon

Business hours: 6:00PM - 11:00PM

General Manager: Stephane Colling, *Executive Chef:* Yosuke Suga

Pastry chef: Rick Billings, *Director of Wine:* Emilie Garvey

Groups (max. group size): 6

Payment: Amex, Mastercard, Visa, Diners, *Price:* $100 And up per person

Food Ratings: 1 Michelin Star, Zagat, Food: 27 Service: 26
New York Times 3 Stars

Reservations: First 6 pm seating at counter, reservations required; thereafter no reservations; table seating requires reservations all evening

Dress Code: Appropriate casual

Architecture: I. M. Pei-designed hotel, *Interior Design:* Pierre Yves Rochon

Additional features: valet parking is available; wheelchair accessible; named Best New Restaurant of the Year – 2007 James Beard Foundation, listed among top ten restaurants in NYC in the Zagat Restaurant Survey

From top left to bottom right:
- La Langoustine
  Fresh langoustine carpaccio with toasted poppy seeds
- L' Amadai
  Pan sauteed amadai served in a lily bulb broth
- Le Ris de Veau
  Sweetbreads with a sprig of fresh laurel and stuffed romaine lettuce
- Les Herbes
  Pineapple vanilla coulis, Chartreuse sabayon, aromatic herb sorbet

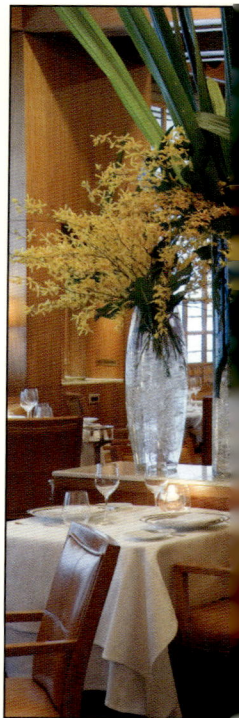

Le Bernardin

155 West 51st Street (Between 6th and 7th Avenues)

Le Bernardin

Address: 155 West 51st Street, New York, NY 10019
(Between 6th and 7th Avenues)
Phone: (212) 554 1515, *Fax:* (212) 554 1100
Internet: www.le-bernardin.com

Cuisine: Seafood

Chef-Owner: Eric Ripert, *Owner:* Maguy Le Coze

Business hours: 12:00PM - 2:30PM, Saturday no lunch
5:15PM - 10:30PM, Fri and Sat 5:15PM - 11:00PM, Closed Sunday

Closed: (Vacation) We are closed on Sundays and major holidays

General Manager: David Mancini

Executive Chef: Eric Ripert, *Pastry chef:* Michael Laiskonis

Maître d'Hôtel: Ben Chekroun, *Wine Director:* Aldo Sohm

Groups (max. group size): 10 people

Private Dining: yes, Karin Burroughs is the contact 212-554-1108
(Les Salons Bernardin)

Payment: Amex, Mastercard, Visa, Diners

Price: We are prix-fixe, Lunch is $66 per person (3 courses). Dinner $109
per person (4 courses). Tasting Menus start at $135 per person.

Food Ratings: 3 Michelin Star, top rated by Zagat for food for years, Food
4 stars New York Times

Reservations: required, *Dress Code:* jacket required; ties are optional

Interior Design: Phil & Gail George

From top left to bottom right:
• Marinated Hamachi Vietnamese Style, Nuoc Mam Vinaigrette
• Sauteed Calamari Filled with Sweet Prawns and Wood Ear Mushroom
  Calamari Consomme
• Barely Cooked Organic Scottish Salmon; Water Chestnuts and Pea Tendrils;
  Gingered Baby Bok Choi and Citrus Emulsion
• Yuzu Parfait, Meringue, Green Tea Biscuit and Ice Cream

Food and wine pairing: a new approach

Have you ever found yourself in the situation of having prepared a tasty dish only to find that it ruins the taste of a perfect wine?
Have you ever wondered why a particular dish or wine tastes good in summer, yet fails the taste test in winter?
Have you ever noticed that wines produced by different wine growers in a particular region, and made from the same grape varieties, do not taste the same?
Have you ever asked yourself why communicating about taste and flavor needs to be so difficult?

Chances are you have, and this, in turn, may have led you to determine that taste is a matter of personal preference. This being the case, you may consider efforts to address the dynamics of food and wine to be somewhat frivolous, and you certainly wouldn't be the only one to think so.

I, however, beg to differ. About ten years ago, I came to the realization that what we needed was a new approach that would give us the answers we need in order to understand the essence of flavor and the practice of pairing food and wines. In developing this new approach, it became clear to me that we have traditionally looked at the issue from the wrong perspective. The new insights I have gleaned will help us to understand the complex world of flavor in general, and offer exciting possibilities to the wide world of food preparation in all of its many guises. They constitute a part of what we now refer to as "flavor theory."

New concepts
The new approach demands new concepts. A central concept of the new flavor theory is the "flavor profile".

In order to understand what this is, we must first define what we mean by "flavor" and that, in turn, can only be understood in relation to "taste". Taste is one of the five senses with which humans are endowed. People have the capacity to taste the flavor of foods and drinks.

As one of the five senses, taste is profoundly linked to the other senses. Our tongue, nose and eyes are all involved in the act of tasting, thus taste is inextricably bound up with the senses of touch, smell and sight. Once we have placed "taste" into this human context, we can move on to say that "flavor" is the counterpart of taste. Where taste belongs to the taster, if you will, flavor is exclusively associated with the food products, themselves.

All foods and drinks have flavor. Flavor can be broken down into a number of separate elements: the gustatory element, the olfactory element and the tactile element. Though broader in definition than most dictionaries, its natural consequence is worth looking at more closely.

A conscious awareness of the distinction between taste and flavor is very useful. Taste, being linked to humans, is by definition a subjective concept. People have different capacities, experience and culture and they experience taste in their particular environments. This will necessarily influence the registration of flavor, but it certainly doesn't influence the nature of the flavor itself.

Compare this to the idea of color. The color of a given object will remain steadfast, even though it may be experienced differently by people with varying degrees of visual ability. Likewise, flavor is objective. To avoid subjectivity when defining a flavor, the tasting of the food item in question must be undertaken by a team of tasters.

Once all of this has been established, we need descriptors: parameters or rather concepts that can be used to describe flavor. In the field of physics, frequency (hertz) and intensity (decibel) are the parameters used to describe the phenomenon of sound. In the field of flavor, "mouthfeel" and "flavor richness" are the parameters we use to help us define flavors.

Mouthfeel
Humans are, from birth, highly sensitive with regard to mouthfeel. There is no flavor without mouthfeel. It can be defined as: the human perception of the texture of food or beverage in the mouth. Mouthfeel covers all tactile experiences, including texture, thermal effects and chemical influences of acids, salts, minerals, metals and irritants.

Mouthfeel is closely related to food appreciation. Toasted bread that has lost its crispness will have lost much of its appeal as well. In the process of wine-making, wine growers will traditionally counterbalance a highly acidic wine by adding alcohol or residual sugar; otherwise it will develop into an unappealing wine. As a tool to aid us in describing particular flavors, mouthfeel can be subdivided into two categories: coating and contracting.

Coating mouthfeel
Creamy, fatty substances and those containing a significant amount of dissolved sugars, coat the mouth. In other words, they leave a layer of fat or sugar behind. These substances also influence saliva by making it thicker. In beverages, alcohol and sugars are viscous, coating elements. They coat the mouth, and this coating may influence the way in which the mouth perceives the next mouthful of food it encounters. Proteins also produce a coating mouthfeel, especially amino acids and some chemical substitutions like gelatin.

Contracting mouthfeel
Acidity and saltiness play an important part in the composition of many foods, and trigger a contracting response in the mouth. The papillae on the tongue register the presence of acidity and saltiness; this is experienced as tactile "tingling" or "stinging" impressions. The acidic wine will have a "contracting" mouthfeel, as will the freshness of a green salad, citrus fruit, apples, and pickles. No wonder such wines go well with salads and other fresh foods.

Frozen substances such as can be found in ice cream also trigger a fresh and tingling oral sensation. They have a rinsing, refreshing influence in the mouth. In fact, the pores located in the mouth contract to bring about this effect. The more extreme tactile reactions produced by CO_2, menthol, raw onion, mustard, ginger, horseradish and some peppers are similar to the reactions triggered by milder foodstuffs, but they are very different from a chemical and physiological point of view. The common denominator is that all of these food substances trigger a contracting, prickling or stinging feeling.

Contracting mouthfeel may also be characterized by dryness in the mouth. Foodstuffs that easily absorb saliva can cause this: a dry biscuit, a crispy, fresh crust of bread, potato chips, some meats and nuts. The drying (roughing, puckering) effect in the mouth caused by tannins (red wine) and other bitter tasting elements (as in coffee, tea or unsweetened chocolate) is also characteristic of contracting mouthfeel.

Contracting mouthfeel and coating mouthfeel are capable of neutralizing each other. Oil (coating) and vinegar (contracting) are mixed together to create a well-balanced vinaigrette. Alcohol and/or residual sugar (coating) balances/neutralizes the acidity (contracting) of wines. A dry slice of toast (contracting) will neutralize a slice of smoked salmon (coating). The fattiness of that smoked salmon may also be neutralized by teaming it up with lemon, raw onion or horseradish, all of which trigger a contracting mouthfeel.

Flavor richness
The decibel and the lux are units of measure used to plot sound and light intensity, respectively. Flavor richness is their counterpart in the field of flavor. As with contracting mouthfeel and coating mouthfeel, flavor richness can be scaled from low to high. The level of flavor richness can be classified by regarding the flavor type.

Flavors that are characterized by the fresh, fruity, acidic tones of lemons, apples and menthol are called fresh. Such flavors are easily associated with spring and summer. Primary fruit flavors in general are often fresh, as are herbs like chives, parsley, chervil, and mint. Fennel, leek, raw onion and raw peppers are examples of vegetables that bring freshness to dishes.

As flavor richness increases, ripe flavor tones are likely to increase. Consider the changes that occur in the flavor profile of a potato depending on whether it is boiled, pan fried or deep-fried. Frying or grilling meat or fish shows how flavor intensity rises, while the flavor type changes to ripe. This is also true of onions and peppers that are roasted in the oven. Other examples of food ingredients with ripe flavor tones are mushrooms, caramel and vanilla. In wine-making, the process known as barrel aging will bring about differences in flavor style, giving such wines a ripe character, just as aging does. In many cases flavor intensity and ripe flavor tones rise with the level of preparation, leading to higher levels of flavor richness. Pure and non-prepared foods are likely to be lower in flavor richness.

Flavor profile

Foods and drinks can be classified with the three above-mentioned parameters. Contracting mouthfeel, coating mouthfeel and flavor richness can all be scaled from low to high. The three-dimensional model below is called the flavor styles cube.

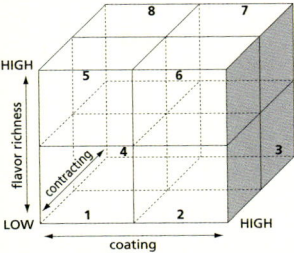

The Flavor Styles Cube

The world of flavor is a cube. Classified products find their place somewhere in this world based on their perceived objective properties. This basic structure can easily be subdivided into eight flavor-style categories:

FLAVOR STYLE	PRIMARY FLAVOR FACTORS		
	CONTRACTING	COATING	FLAVOR RICHNESS
1. NEUTRAL	Low	Low	Low
2. ROUND	Low	High	Low
3. BALANCE LOW	High	High	Low
4. FRESH	High	Low	Low
5. POWERFUL/DRY	Low	Low	High
6. RICH	Low	High	High
7. BALANCE HIGH	High	High	High
8. PUNGENT	High	Low	High

Practical use

The empirical model of the new flavor theory is scientifically validated in my academic thesis "The Concept of Flavor Styles in the Classification of Flavors", for which I received my PhD in 2004. Unfortunately, the consumer version "Het Proefboek, de essentie van smaak" is at the moment only available in Dutch. This book is widely used by food professionals and educators in The Netherlands. It was touted as best

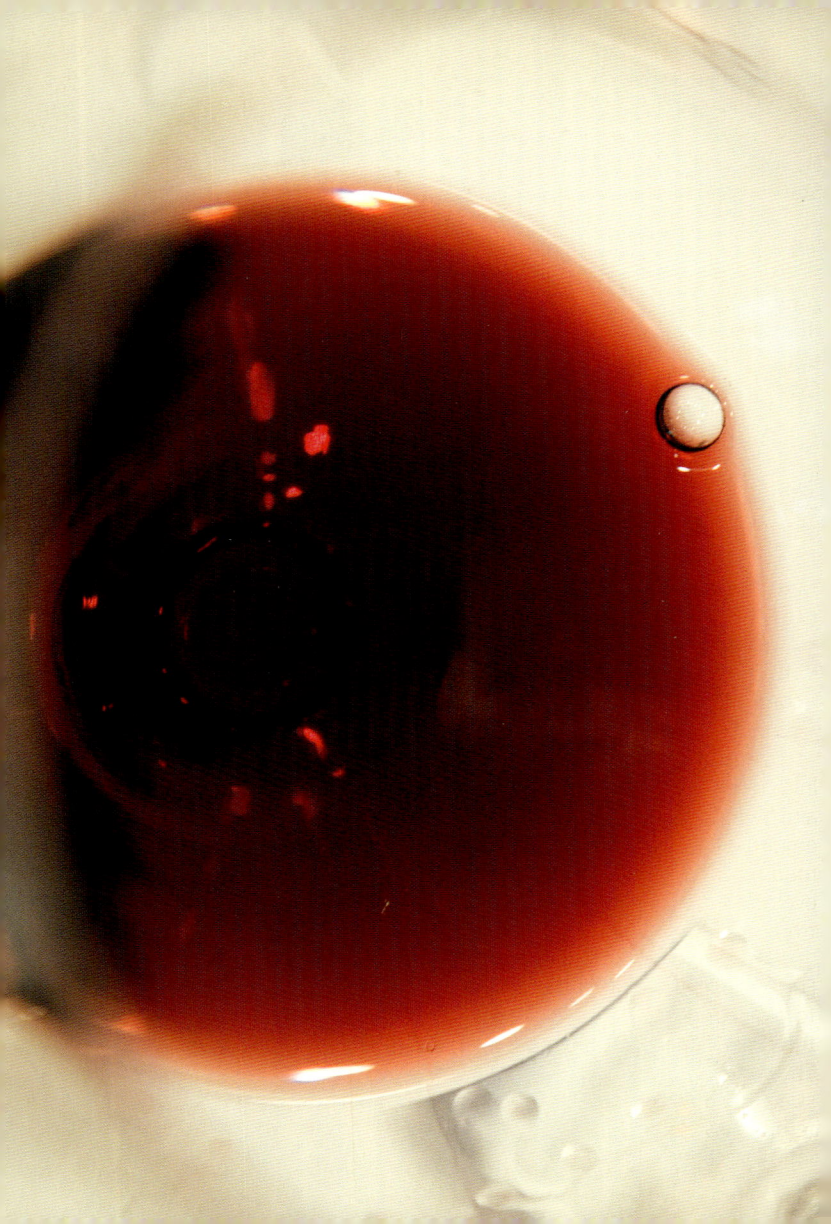

book for food professionals by World Gourmand Cookbook Awards 2004. In Holland, Belgium and Denmark the theory has been widely adopted.

New gastronomic guidelines
Space in this book is limited, so instead of elaborating on the flavor styles, allow me to address some of the advantages of this new flavor theory. Indeed, it has proven to be very useful in daily practice.

A big advantage of the new flavor theory is that it is a universal language that is easy to comprehend. In our courses we do not need much time to get people to understand how a flavor profile can be determined. Consequently the guidelines for wine and food pairing have proven to be very useful and relatively easy to apply. Flavor is what wines and food have in common. Thus, the same descriptors can be used. This leads to new guidelines for the paring of food and wine. Basically, good combinations are found if the flavor profile of wines and foods resemble one another. In other words:

• Contracting wines go well with contracting foods
• Coating wines go well with coating foods
• The flavor richness of wines and foods should be about the same
• The rule of thumb when composing a menu is to progress from contracting to coating foods and wines, and from lower levels of flavor richness to higher levels.

In this new flavor theory, the color of the wine, grape varieties, region and year are not important; the new theory goes beyond traditional emphases on wine labels and menu descriptions of food. Instead new roads are opened, roads that were previously considered to be closed or even non-existent. Creativity in gastronomy is enhanced when it grows from a solid base.

Furthermore it becomes clear that small changes in preparation will lead to big changes in flavor. Amounts of salt and various herbs, acidity, the thickness of a sauce, will all, in their own way, change the flavor profile. The same applies to wines: such things as the use of a particular yeast strain, a change in the length of the vinification period, variation of temperature during fermentation and the use of wooden barrels will influence the flavor profile of wine. This explains why wines do not all taste the same even though they come from the same region, year and grape variety.

Culinary Success Factors
Another interesting application of the new flavor theory is the formulation of culinary success factors. We searched for factors that determine palatability, which we define as flavors that are pleasing to the palate. The term "palatable" is easily confused with "liking", which is defined as the human response to a certain flavor. As such, "liking" is a subjective concept. Palatability on the other hand, is product-related, and can be considered to be a successful combination of product characteristics. In order for a restaurant dish to be considered palatable, it must exhibit all of the following six characteristics:
1. the name and presentation must fit the expectation
2. the aroma should be appetizing and appropriate to the food
3. there should be a good balance of flavor components in relation to the food
4. the savory, "deliciousness" factor, umami (also called the fifth basic taste), must be present
5. the mouthfeel of the dish should offer a mix of hard and soft textures
6. it must be characterized by high flavor richness.

It is interesting to note that one hospital in Denmark has evaluated and changed all of its recipes based on these factors. Patient satisfaction with regard to food has risen so much that the method is currently being applied in 14 other hospitals.

Conclusion
If my good friend, Jan Bartelsman, had come to me 10 years ago and asked me to write a chapter on my new flavor theory for his book, I would have hesitated. At that time I had just presented the new ideas, and nobody could foresee the impact it would have.
However, in the Netherlands, today, terms like "coating mouthfeel", "contracting mouthfeel" and "flavor richness" are bandied about very casually in restaurants, wine shops and magazines. Supermarket magazines, several food industries and many journalists have also adopted the new flavor-language. The new theory is implemented in educational programs on various levels. The sommelier training in the Netherlands is based on the theory and many chefs use it to their advantage.

Most recently, Wageningen University, one of the leading European universities in the field of Life Sciences, has begun to develop a new Master of Science program for gastronomy.
All these activities will hopefully lead to a wider adoption of the flavor styles theory.

Cheers,

Peter Klosse, PhD

About the author

Peter Klosse was born February 3, 1956. In 1983 he continued his parents' restaurant, "De Echoput", which was awarded its first Michelin star in 1967.
In 1991, he founded the Academy for Gastronomy, which offers professional courses in wine and food pairing, based on the flavor theory he developed. He has published several commercially successful books on this subject. The version for food professionals of his doctoral thesis is called "Het Proefboek", currently available only in Dutch. In 2008, in collaboration with photographer Jan Bartelsman, he published "Chef en Sommelier," which shows how some of the best chefs and sommeliers in The Netherlands work and apply the new flavor theory.
Meanwhile, his restaurant, De Echoput, continues to be successful. In 2004, it closed its doors for a time, reopening in 2007 as a five star luxury design hotel. The restaurant was chosen as best new luxury restaurant in 2008 by the IRHA (International Restaurant and Hotel Awards).

Hotel Gastronomique De Echoput - Academie voor Gastronomie
Amersfoortseweg 86
NL-7346 AA Hoog Soeren (the Netherlands)

www.echoput.nl
www.academiegastronomie.nl

Milos
125 West 55th Street (between 6th and 7th Avenues)

Milos

Address: 125 West 55th Street, New York, NY 10019
(Between 6th and 7th avenues)
Phone: (212) 245 7400, *Fax:* (212) 245 4828
Internet: www.milos.ca

Cuisine: Fresh Fish and Seafood, Mediterranean style

Chef-Owner: Costas Spiliadis

Business hours: 12:00PM - 3:00PM Sun no lunch,
5:00PM - 11:45PM, 5:00PM - 10:45PM Sun

Chef: Mohiuddin Jahangir Alam

Maître d'Hôtel: Mario Zeniou

Wine Director: Michael Coll

Private Dining: 2 rooms: 24 + 12

Payment: Amex, Mastercard, Visa, Diners

Price: $ 73 and up

Food Ratings: 1 Michelin Star, Zagat, Food 26, Service 23

Reservations: accepted

Dress Code: business, New York casual

Interior Design: Costas Spiliadis & Charles Morris Mount

Notable features: Sister restaurants in Montreal + Athens.

From top left to bottom right:
- Milos Special: Paper-thin Zucchini,eggplant and Saganaki cheese, lighty fried
- Octopus: Sashimi quality Mediterranean Octopus-broiled
- Red Snapper: Pensacola. White meat

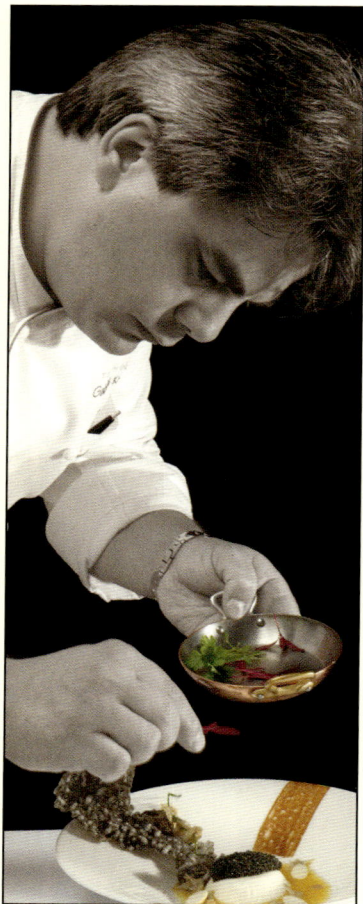

The Modern
9 West 53rd Street (between 5th and 6th Avenues)

The Modern

Address: 9 West 53rd Street NY, NY 10019
(Between 5th and 6th Avenues)
Phone: 212.333.1220, *Fax:* 212.408.6322
Internet: www.themodernnyc.com, email: info@themodernnyc.com

Cuisine: French-American

Chef-Owner: Union Square Hospitality Group

Business hours: Bar Room: 11:30AM - 10:30PM 7 days a week;
Dining Room: Lunch Mon-Fri, Dinner Mon-Sat, Closed Sunday

Closed: Thanksgiving and Christmas

General Manager: Graceanne Jordan, *Executive Chef:* Gabriel Kreuther

Pastry chef: Marc Aumont, *Wine Steward:* Belinda Chang

Groups (max. group size): 8

Private Dining: Yes

Payment: Amex, Mastercard, Visa, Diners

Price: $125 and up per person

Food Ratings: 1 Michelin Star, 26 Zagat: Food, 26 Service 24,
3 Stars New York Times

Reservations: Recommended. Also available through website.

Dress Code: Jacket required in Dining room for dinner.

Architecture: Peter Bentel & Paul Bentel

Interior Design: Bauhaus

Additional features: Wheelchair access; Best New Restaurant 2006 –
James Beard Foundation

From top left to bottom:
- Almond Panna Cotta with Yellowstone River Caviar, Cockle Clams, and Orange Emulsion
- Chorizo-Crusted Codfish with White Coco Bean Puree and Harissa Oil
- Heirloom Tomato Terrine with Tomato-Melon Soup and Tomato Sorbet
- Lemon Napoleon, Exotique Fruit "Brunoise" and "Fromage Blanc" Sorbet

Nobu
105 Hudson Street (on the corner of Franklin and Hudson Streets)

Nobu

Address: 105 Hudson Streets, New York, NY 10013
(on the corner of Franklin and Hudson Street)
Phone: (212) 219 0500, *Fax:* (212) 219 1441
Internet: www.noburestaurants.com

Cuisine: New Style Japanese

Chef-Owner: Nobu Matsuhisa

Business hours: 11:45AM - 2:15PM No lunch Sat & Sun,
Dinner 5:45PM - 10:15PM

Closed: (Vacation) major holidays

General Manager: Hiro Tahara

Executive Chef: Ricky Estrellado Executive

Sushi Chef: Tosho Tomita, *Pastry Chef:* Jessica Isaacs

Groups (max. group size): 10

Private Dining: Back Room 50 guests standing and 40 guests seated,
Entire Restaurant 220 guests standing and 140 guests seated

Payment: Amex, Mastercard, Visa, Diners, Discover

Price: $80 and up per person

Food Ratings: 27 Zagat Food, 3 stars New York Times

Service Ratings: 23 Zagat

Reservations: Highly recommended, Sushi Bar available for walk in

Dress Code: Smart Casual

Architecture/Interior Design: David Rockwell

Additional features: wheelchair access

From top left to bottom right:
- Sashimi Salad with Matsuhisa Dressing
- Scallop Tiradito Nobu Style
- Broiled Black Cod with Miso
- Soft Shell Crab Roll

Maestro Nobu

We have been very lucky in our work. As publicists for cookbooks from some of the greatest chefs in the world, we get to see them in ways many others don't. Most people experience the work of the celebrity chef only through the cooking of their highly trained staffs in one of the restaurant locations in many cities of the world.

The celebrity chefs train their chefs and management staff extremely well and then leave them to the run the restaurants, while they spend most of their time traveling the world, visiting their locations, developing new concepts and scoping out new locations for expanding their empire.

No one typifies this type of global celebrity chef more than Nobu Matsuhisa. With restaurants in New York, Tokyo, Dubai, London, Los Angeles, Aspen, Miami and Milan, you'd have more luck meeting Nobu on a plane than in one of his restaurants, which are some of the best in the world. The secret is Nobu's training and management and his extraordinary ability to appear in many places at once.

In 2001, Nobu's publisher, Kodansha International, hired us to promote his first cookbook, Nobu: The Cookbook. We couldn't have been more excited at the prospect of helping Nobu sell cookbooks by booking him on television shows and securing interviews about the book in newspapers across the country.

We were able to secure a major feature in The New York Times right at publication. For a book launch, this is major coup. For the story, Nobu would cook four of his signature recipes for a reporter and be photographed, with articles running for four consecutive weeks.

We were excited and nervous, too. While we had worked with Nobu for six months, we'd actually never seen him cook. Of course we knew he could cook, we just had never seen it. When the day came for the interview, Nobu arrived with his knife kit and all of the raw ingredients at the kitchen of Nobu Next Door in New York City.

The reporter took out her notebook and Nobu began to sharpen his knives. From the second he opened the bag, we knew we were in the presence of a true master. The room fell silent, with the whirring of the knife against the steel the only sound we heard.

The knives were Japanese - extremely long, thin and sharp. After they were sharpened to Nobu's satisfaction, he grabbed a large piece of fish and began slicing off paper-thin pieces and laying them to the side of his work area. His hands were moving like a symphony conductor's, and within minutes he had a large number of slices. When we looked at them closely, they were all the exact same size, including their thickness! It was as if a computerized robotic hand had sliced the fish. It was nothing short of perfection… and one of the most beautiful things we had ever seen.

We've had the privilege of working with Nobu on other books in the past seven years. We've taken him to The Today Show and Martha and paid a visit to Live with Regis and Kelly, where he wowed the hosts and the audience with his signature dishes.

But with time, the memory of what we witnessed has not dimmed. Underneath all of the fame and hype of the Nobu empire is the hand of a great sushi master.

Kimberly Yorio and Caitlin Friedman

Oceana
55 East 54th Street (Between Park and Madison Avenues)
From August 2009: 1221 Avenue of the Americas

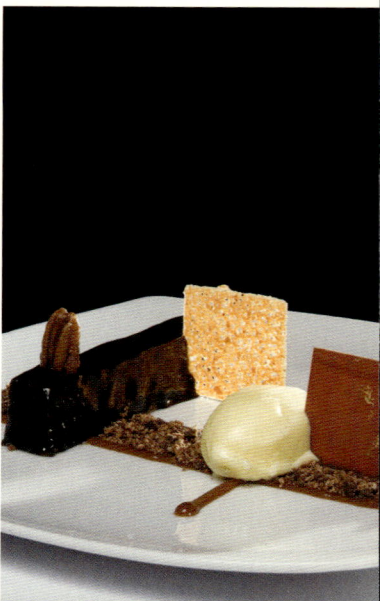

Oceana

Address: 55 East 54th Street, New York, NY 10022
(Between Park and Madison Avenues)
Phone: (212) 759 5941
Internet: www.oceanarestaurant.com

Cuisine: Seafood

Owners: Livanos Family

Business hours: 12:00PM - 2:30PM, 5:30PM - 10:30PM,
Sat. 5:00PM - 10:30PM, Saturday no lunch, closed Sunday

Managing Partner: Paul McLaughlin

Executive chef: Ben Pollinger

Pastry chef: Jansen Chan

Private dining in Wine Cellar: 24 seats, *Upstairs Salon:* 60 seats

Payment: All major credit cards

Price: lunch $33 and up, dinner $78 and up per person

Ratings: 1 Michelin Star, Zagat: Food 26, Service 24

Reservations: Recommended, *Dress Code:* Business casual attire

Architecture and Design: Morris Nathanson

Notable features: Restaurant designed to resemble a luxury cruise ship.
From August 2009: 1221 Avenue of the Americas

From top left to bottom right:
- Taro Wrapped Pompano
  Baby Bok Choy, Long Beans, Peanuts, Basmati Rice, Coconut Cilantro Curry
- Sautéed Sea Scallops
  Mamey, Citrus Salad, Charoli Nuts
- Frozen Banana Mousse
  Sticky Lemon Rice, Black Pepper Meringue
- "Chocolate Chip - Pecan Cookie" Bar
  Buttermilk Ice Cream

Where the bufala roam

Vogue, September 2003

You may have to be brave to run with the bulls of Pamplona, but to roam with the water buffalo of southern Italy, as Jeffrey Steingarten does, you must also be crazy – for mozzarella di bufala.

Thank you, Baroness," I said as I discreetly peeled a juicy wedge of zucchini frittata from the front of my shirt, on which it had somehow fallen, while with the other hand I accepted a deep-blue oval dish holding one of the two peerless treasures for which we had traveled to Italy. It was a plump, glistening, porcelain-white piece of buffalo-milk mozzarella. It had been made earlier that day at a local dairy and was in the form of a braid.

"A trecce," I exclaimed, hoping to demonstrate to the baroness my deep knowledge of culinary Italian but in my excitement mistakenly using the plural for braid. Yes, I was overwrought. But who can blame me? Mozzarella di bufala, mozzarella cheese made from the milk of the water buffalo, is the original mozzarella (or so I thought), the finest and most delicious, now esteemed the world over. This was Peerless Treasure Number One.

And here we were, fewer than 24 hours after leaving New York City, having dinner on an actual water-buffalo farm, Azienda Agrituristica Seliano. It is owned by Cecilia Baratta Bellelli, an extremely handsome and magnetic woman who makes nothing of her title, baronessa, which came from her late husband, as did the farm itself. (She did, though, show me a printed version of the Bellelli family portrait by Degas that hangs in the Musée d'Orsay; Degas's aunt was a Bellelli.) Cecilia has developed the farm as an agriturismo, where paying guests can stay in one of the fourteen rooms or just come to dine. To qualify for government tax subsidies, agriturismos must satisfy a series of requirements; among them, half the food served has to be grown on the farm. In Cecilia's case, the number is as high as 70 percent. We were surrounded by fields of artichokes, and our lunches and dinners – all taken outdoors under a wooden shed roof, sometimes along with dozens of other guests – were composed of delectable vegetable dishes, eggs, and pasta, and not much meat. Cecilia's 600 water buffalo live about ten minutes away on her other piece of farmland, Masseria Eliseo.

Early that morning, exhausted but glowing with expectation, my assistant, Elizabeth, a putative Italophone, and I had landed at Rome's Fiumicino airport. Our glow was only briefly dulled when the attendants at Thrifty Rental Car, a man and a woman, let us know that the automobile we had ordered a month earlier and had confirmed an hour before leaving Manhattan would not be ready for two days. When I saw that Elizabeth was refusing to pass on my observations regarding the mental and physical shortcomings of the Thrifty staff and their extended families, justifiably feeling betrayed I abandoned her to her two new Italian friends, and within fifteen minutes found the same car at a rental outfit across the room for only twice the price.

Then we were hurtling down the autostrada. Blissfully air-conditioned against what CNN had called the worst Italian heat wave in a century, we headed south from Rome and into the region of Campania, one of 20 governmental regioni that make up Italy and the undisputed world capital of mozzarella di bufala. We bypassed Naples, Vesuvius, and Pompeii, the Sorrento peninsula, and the city of Salerno and steered south to Cecilia's farm, which lies between the towns of Capaccio Scalo and Paestum, near the coast. Within minutes we were in the embrace of my old friend Arthur Schwartz. Apart from being New York's leading food-radio personality (www. arthurschwartz.com), Arthur is a great expert on Naples and the rest of Campania. His book Naples at Table (HarperCollins) is an invaluable, charming source of recipes, lore, and crucial information, and four times a year he and Cecilia teach weeklong cooking courses for Americans at the Azienda Agrituristica Seliano. Thus it was not by chance that we found ourselves together on this day.

Soon dinner was upon us, and with Baronessa Cecilia at the head of the table, on my immediate right, I cut out a center section of the treccia and got ready for my first taste in seven years of the real thing. Yes, you can easily find imported mozzarella di bufala at expensive Italian groceries and restaurants in the United States. But connoisseurs will tell you that nothing deserves the name but the handmade mozzarella of Campania. For one thing, they say, mozzarella, especially if it is made with buffalo milk, must be eaten on the day it is produced, before the flavors fade and the texture softens and disintegrates. Plus, the best buffalo mozzarella in Campania uses unpasteurized (or raw) milk, which would be illegal here under FDA regulations. Raw milk is more flavorful in itself, and it contains enzymes and micro-organisms that can develop complex flavors in cheese.

I chewed a piece of treccia, in a ruminative manner, not unlike that of the beast that made it possible. So this was buffalo mozzarella! It was very firm, even slightly rubbery. It squeaked a little against my teeth. It was juicy but not creamy or even buttery. It had the taste and aroma of cooked milk and cream, and the muskiness of buffalo milk. It was also brightly acidic and salty. You might have called it spongy. The cheese was compact but shot through with tiny holes, like tufa, as one book describes it, like volcanic rock. And when I squeezed it, liquid oozed, not thick like heavy cream but milky and translucent. The name for this substance, we later learned, is latticello.

My first sample of genuine mozzarella di bufala in seven years was not luscious, not even succulent, though it was very good to eat. But what if I ended up preferring the false, pasteurized, degenerate, soft, dripping version of mozzarella I have gotten used to in the United States? How many times have I been forced to listen while people told me, on their return from foreign parts, that they prefer American pizza to the stuff you find in Naples, or that they can't stand the Chinese food in China? And how many times have I put these people's names and thumbnail photos on my secret and ineradicable list of doomed and damaged souls whose opinions about food will no longer be allowed to enter my consciousness?

"The people in Naples like their mozzarella di bufala a little softer," Cecilia explained, "the way it will become by tomorrow." Unlike the cow's-milk version, water-buffalo mozzarella becomes squishier as time passes. If my tastes turned out to be more like those of a resident of nearby Naples than of Capaccio Scalo, I would not need to enter my name and image on the secret list, condemned never again to talk to myself about food. And this in the end proved to be the case. There were no such moral struggles concerning buffalo-milk ricotta, which, still warm from the making, is one of the most delicious foods that humans have ever concocted, strong and sweet with the cooked taste of water-buffalo milk, fragile and trembling on the fork as you bring it to your mouth. All questions, all aesthetic confusion, were banished.

Elizabeth and I drove around the neighborhood to several much-admired dairies. (In this and many other aspects of our trip, we relied on advice and introductions from Faith Willinger, who is hard at work on a food-lover's guide to southern Italy to supplement Eating in Italy [Morrow], her indispensable guide to the north). The town of Capaccio and its surroundings appear to contain more buffalo mozzarella caseifici – dairies where cheese is made – than any square mile or two in the world, and the main drag is a long string of gaudy signs for real and genuine handmade mozzarella di bufala. Returning to the countryside, we paid a brief visit to the widely esteemed Caseificio Rivabianca, then drove just beyond it to the famous organic-buffalo farm and dairy known as Azienda Biologica Vannulo, to which we had been invited for lunch.

It was here that I got to hug a buffalo. "Bubalus," I murmured to one of the larger cows during her lunchtime at the feeding trough, uttering not an affectionate Eastern European diminutive but the very word for water buffalo wherever literary Latin is spoken. And she presented her head for stroking! Soon her friends jostled for a pat on their vast, bristly, black snouts. Like all milking buffalo, these are of a docile Indian breed, not the aggressive, savage, scary-looking African beasts with huge, elaborately curved horns that are, or were, hunted as wild game.

Azienda Biologica Vannulo had apparently been an ordinary buffalo farm for nearly 100 years before the owners began making their own mozzarella in 1988, under the direction of our host, owner Antonio Palmieri, and went organic in 1996. Nearly all the land is planted with organic crops for feeding the buffalo, and the standards of humane treatment of the animals are extremely high, as far as I can judge the matter – nice, green rubber mats in their sleeping stalls, refreshing shower sprays during the day, things like that. Vannulo sells all its products right on the farm – the cheeses from a shop at one end of the cheesemaking room and the fabulously delicious buffalo-milk ice creams and yogurts in a little caffé. Lunch with Signore Palmieri in the family's bougainvillea-covered house – within sight of the dairy – was a delight, climaxing in dessert: a brioche – flat, like a hamburger bun, in the style

I associate with Palermo – sliced in two and filled with buffalo-milk hazelnut ice cream topped with buffalo-milk whipped cream.

However did the Indian water buffalo wind up in Italy? All you read are theories, none of which I am in a position to evaluate. The water buffalo "may have arrived from Asia in the eleventh century," says one source. "Indian buffaloes were first introduced in the sixteenth century, to Campania, Apulia, Basilicata… and to Latium," says another. According to one legend, buffalo were transplanted here by Hannibal, who wanted the milk to nourish his ailments. And from several other authorities: "From Sicily in the South, buffalo reached the fertile wetlands of the plain of Naples where, like pigs in muck, they thrived"; and finally, "Mediterranean buffaloes are autochthonous," meaning indigenous. I've left out the theory that water buffalo were brought along during the invasion of the Longobards because that would mean figuring out who the Longobards were.

Nonetheless, it was a genius idea to import the water buffalo, which did well as draft animals in the sweltering weather and swampy, pestilential land south of Naples and gave the richest, most delicious milk of all. Water-buffalo milk is thicker and more nutritious than cow's milk, containing less water and more solids, more protein and fat, and slightly more sugar – even though the buffalo make do with poorer forage than the dairy cow. India is the world's largest producer – 60 percent of the milk there comes from the water buffalo and is either drunk straight or made into yogurt. Bet you didn't know that.

Cecilia sells all her buffalo milk to a small, artisanal cheesemaker called Azienda Agricola Barlotti, and it was on a long morning's visit there that we learned something about how to make mozzarella di bufala. The methods used at Barlotti (and Vannulo) are largely traditional, though the rooms are lined with white tiles and nearly everything is handled with or in stainless steel. Most of the workers were men, all wearing white T-shirts, white pants, white rubber boots, and white aprons.

They started with unpasteurized buffalo milk, collected an hour or two earlier and poured into a large, round, stainless-steel tank that holds several hundred quarts. The milk, still warm from the milking, was heated to 37 degrees centigrade – which is also the body temperature of both humans and buffalo, not a coincidence if you ask me. They stirred in a vial of animal rennet, a liquid mixture of the enzymes found in the stomach of a suckling calf (there are vegetarian substitutes). And at that precise temperature, one of the proteins in the milk – the casein – clumped, coagulated, in about 20 minutes.

This is the first step in nearly all cheesemaking. The clumps are called curds, and the liquid they were now floating in is called whey. Whey is sweet and nutritious, contains several other milk proteins besides casein, and has very little fat. Most of the fat in the buffalo milk was now held in the casein web that makes up the curds. What distinguishes the thousands of cheeses around the world is everything that is done to the curds after they clump.

Back at Barlotti, the curds had formed a thick, gelatinous layer in the tank, with the vaguely greenish whey underneath. (The tank was four feet high; the curd measured about a foot thick, and the whey three feet deep below it.) Now one of the workers cut the curds into cubes, and a while later with a spino, a large metal whisk, into pieces the size of hazelnuts. Each time, more whey spilled out of the curds, which quickly came together into a mass again. Finally this was portioned up with knives into large slabs, more than a foot on each side, and lifted off to a slanted, stainless-steel table for draining and four hours of ripening. The whey was reserved for at least two other uses, as we'll soon see.

Why does the curd need to ripen? A totally essential question. The answer is that it needs to develop acidity, which changes the structure of the calcium in the casein and makes it stretchable (the pH must be 5.2), which as we'll see is what puts mozzarella and related cheeses into a category of their own. In lactic-acid fermentation, bacteria (lactobacilli) convert the lactose (the main milk sugar) in the curd into lactic acid and carbon dioxide.

At Barlotti and Vannulo and many artisanal mozzarella-makers, the fermentation is kicked off by adding some whey from yesterday's cheesemaking at the very start of the process. Besides acidifying the curd, this helps reproduce that particular dairy's characteristic flavors. It's like leavening sourdough bread or pain au levain by starting with a piece of yesterday's dough rather than adding a package of yeast. There are at least two other ways to make the curds acidic. The easiest is to pour some vinegar or citric acid right into the milk. Most cow's-milk mozzarella produced in the United States is made this way. The result is an unnaturally sweet cheese – without fermentation, the lactose never gets converted into lactic acid and remains simply sweet – often with a background taste of vinegar. The second is through fermentation using a standardized, purchased cheese culture, which can produce reliable results every time. But a standardized bacterial culture will produce standardized flavors.

When the three or four hours of fermentation had passed, one of the men fed the curd into a cutting machine that reduced the huge pieces of tofu-looking material into little strips. Then he took the little strips and put them in a large steel bowl, while another man poured boiling water over them and a third started stirring with a wooden pole – sometimes adding boiling water, more often removing it as it cooled. And miraculously, in five to ten minutes, the pieces of curd had melted together into a beautiful, glossy mass that looked like Italian meringue or wet bread dough being kneaded, as the worker continued to stretch it with a circular motion. (It is now known as the "pasta," an Italian word for dough, like the French word "pâté.") In larger mozzarella dairies, the stirring and stretching are done by machine. Most people will tell you, though, that no machine has been invented that can mimic the skill of the workers at Barlotti.

Now the individual mozzarellas were formed, with three workers standing together over a rectangular tank of cold water. Two men took long pieces of mozzarella pasta that had been cut from the mass, folded them on themselves several times, and, squeezing the ends between their thumbs and forefingers, formed shiny little balls that a woman, turning first to one man and then to the other, pulled off and dropped into the cold water. (The smallest shapes were made by machine – the only other example of mechanization in the entire dairy.) Mozzarella comes from the verb "mozzare," meaning to cut or pull off. Before being sold, the various shapes of mozzarella were put in brine for salting.

Most of the leftover whey at Barlotti is used to make ricotta. With the casein gone, other milk proteins remaining in the whey coagulate nicely at temperatures near the boiling point, without the need for rennet, forming little curds, like those in cottage cheese but smaller. Made like this, ricotta is a very economical product to prepare. Warm buffalo-milk ricotta is one of the finest things you can eat. In fact, I'd say it is even more delicious than buffalo-milk mozzarella.

Cecilia put us in touch with Dottore Roberto Rubino, and we drove down to Basilicata (the regione just south of Campania) to meet him. In a word, or two words, Rubino is Mr. Cheese, and we had already encountered his name and his work all over the place. He is a director of the Istituto Sperimentale per la Zootecnia; head of ANFOSC, which advocates cheese made from milk given by cattle that live and graze outdoors, in aromatic pastures; editorial director of the magazine Caseus; and guiding light behind the essential Mozzarelle di Bufala (Slow Food Arcigola Editore, in Italian only).

Basilicata was unexpectedly mountainous and sublimely beautiful, and in order to prolong our trip from 90 minutes to three times that, we took nearly every wrong turn that presented itself. Elizabeth did the driving. I got us home, in a trice.

Rubino is worried about the quality of milk – everywhere – and the sad irony that today, when so many people are making traditional cheeses by hand again, hardly anybody pays attention to the wild, herby flavors of natural milk. Australia and New Zealand still have good milk, he said, and parts of the French Alps. He fears that even water-buffalo milk is on the decline, as the animals are bred to produce more.

We talked about mozzarella di bufala, and its cow's-milk counterpart, which is officially called fior di latte. Both belong to the category of pasta filata – stringed or threaded or stretched curd. Mozzarella di bufala and fior di latte are the versions intended for immediate consumption; if the stretched curd is prepared in a slightly different manner and then allowed to age and ripen, it becomes scamorza, caciocavallo, provola, or provolone. As cow's-milk caciocavallo was mentioned in the 1300s, and buffalo-milk mozzarella not until the 1400s, Rubino concludes that fior di latte, cow's-milk mozzarella, must be the original.

We asked Dottore Rubino what is the juice, the latticello, that oozes out of a properly juicy mozzarella – the substance people call creamy or buttery or milky. It is simply the hot water in which the mozzarella curd is stretched – or not so simply, because by the end of that process, the latticello contains whey, water, and traces of casein and butterfat.

For lunch, Dottore Rubino served us a delectable local salami and . . . cheeses! Our favorites were a wonderful goat's-milk ricotta made right there at the Istituto and still warm, and a rare DOP cheese, a Caciocavallo Podolico. And what about people who like their mozzarella really squishy and soft? That's simply an error, Rubino said – unless the cheese was prepared with lower acidity than usual so that it would start out superelastic and then improve during shipment. Some people have just never eaten the real thing. Which is what we dined on that evening, back at Cecilia's farm – the real thing.

Soon it was time to say goodbye to Cecilia and Arthur and the buffalo of Paestum, and to set off in pursuit of Peerless Treasure Number Two. Seven years ago at the restaurant Bacco near the city of Bari in the regione of Puglia – directly across the Italian peninsula from Campania – I attended a dinner arranged by Faith at which our first course was a shiny little white pouch sitting alone on a plate. Food writer and friend David Rosengarten was there, too, and in a recent issue of his nine-issue-yearly Rosengarten Report he recalled that same moment. I'll quote his description because if I use my own words, you might think me over-the-top, besotted, and on the edge of madness: "I will never, ever forget that bite: a round of impeccably stretchy, resilient mozzarella which, at the prick of my fork, released a white volcanic flow of creamy ooze from deep inside. I have never in my life tasted deeper, more profound, more ecstatic layers of pure dairy-cream-butter flavor – and may never again."

I second that emotion.

What can you do when you are deeply haunted by a cheese or cheese product? I needed to return to Puglia. We had worked it into our plans months before. And now David's recollection, arriving just before we left for Italy, confirmed that. My epiphanic memory from seven years before was no exaggeration.

And there we were, speeding along yet another autostrada toward the little Adriatic city of Barletta, where the restaurant Bacco has moved and been renamed Baccosteria by its owner and chef, Francesco Ricatti. We had telephoned Franco with Faith's help, and that evening we had a fine meal at his one-Michelin-star restaurant. The next morning we followed Franco to the maker of our first and still most fantastic burrata so many years ago – the Caseificio Andriese, a small storefront producer in Barletta, where everything is done by hand with unpasteurized milk and everything is spotless, all tiles and stainless steel.

The burrata expert, Giuseppe Fortugno, was ready to give us a demonstration. A burrata is a little sack or bag or pouch made out of mozzarella and filled with the freshest cream and the threads and filaments (the lucini) you get in the course of making mozzarella. Burrata is made from cow's milk and is not an ancient cheese – estimates of its age range from 40 to 75 years, with production centered in several nearby towns, especially Corato, which we'd visit later, and Andria. Mr. Fortugno began with a strip of soft mozzarella pasta and the hot latticello in which it had been made in the front of the shop. He pulled half of it apart into filaments about ten inches long and dropped them into a plastic tub of cream. With the other half he formed a little ball of mozzarella, which he immediately poked, stretched, and shaped into a thin-walled pouch with a wide mouth. He dipped the pouch into cold water to solidify it a bit; dropped in a handful of filaments dripping with cream; topped it off with more cream; tied the precious little sack around its mouth with a plastic tie; and dipped it again into cold water. The ratio of mozzarella filaments to cream is always two to one. At last it was time for a taste. Its surface was shiny and soft, the mozzarella was delicate but very stretchy, and when we cut into it the cream and filaments slowly spilled out, tasting wonderfully fresh, sweet raw milk and cream, with the barest tang in the pasta. There is nothing like it, anywhere.

We left laden with burratas, mozzarella, and ricotta and drove off to visit two other producers, one a mechanized factory built by the owner of Andriese, Signore Onofrio Perina, and the other Cooperativo Caseificio Pugliese in the city of Corato, where mozzarella is made by adding citric acid instead of fermenting the curd. They wrap their burratas in long green leaves for the looks of it. We were not impressed.

After spending two weeks consuming genuine mozzarella di bufala three times a day, and the most perfect burrata, we wondered how we would react to the versions that are available in the United States. Would we still prefer our mozzarella mushy and drippy? Could we find anything like the sweet, fresh burrata of Puglia? We undertook to taste every brand sold in this country. For the winners, plus our entire list and tasting notes, please E-mail your requests to bufala@earthlink.net.

Jeffrey Steingarten, author of "The Man who Ate Everything", has been the internationally feared and acclaimed food critic of Vogue magazine for many years. He attended Harvard College, Harvard Law School, the Massachusetts Institute of Technology, and worked for the Harvard Lampoon. Recently he has also become the food correspondent for the online magazine Slate. For essays in this collection, Mr. Steingarten has won countless awards from the James Beard Foundation and the International Association of Culinary Professionals. On Bastille Day, 1994, the French Republic made him a Chevalier in the Order of Merit for his writing on French gastronomy.

Per Se
10 Columbus Circle (Time Warner Center, Fourth Floor)

Per Se

Address: 10 Columbus Circle, Time Warner Center, Fourth Floor,
New York, New York 10019
Phone: (212) 823 9335
Internet: www.perseny.com

Cuisine: Contemporary American cuisine with French influences

Chef-Owner: Thomas Keller, *Chief Operating Officer:* Eric Lilavois

Business hours: 11:30AM - 1:30PM, 5:30PM - 10:00PM
No lunch Monday-Thursday

Director of Operations: Raj Dagstani, *General Manager:* Peter Esmond

Chef de Cuisine: Jonathan Benno, *Executive Pastry chef:* Sébastien Rouxel

Pastry Chef: Elwyn Boyles, *Head Sommelier:* James Hayes

Director of Private Dining and Events: Célia Laurent

Private dining: 10-60, 100 for cocktails, two private rooms available

Payment: Amex, Mastercard, Visa

Prix Fixe: $175 for 5 Course Weekend Lunch Menu Option,
$275 for 9 Course Chef's Tasting Menu or 9 Course Tasting of Vegetables,
Dinner and Lunch, Service is included in price

Ratings: 3 Michelin Stars, Zagat: Food 28, Service 28, NY Times: 4 stars

Reservations: Are taken 2 months to the calendar date and can be made
by either calling (212) 823-9335 or on www.opentable.com

Dress Code: Chic, suit and tie

Designer: Tihany Design, New York, NY

Additional features: Wheelchair access, Parking available
Bar and Salon area.

From top left to bottom:
• White Truffle Oil-infused Custard Ragoût of Black Winter Truffles
• Oysters and Pearls
  Sabayon of Pearl Tapioca with Island Creek Oysters and Osetra Caviar
• Cornet of Marinated Atlantic Salmon Tartare with
  Sweet Red Onion Crème Fraiche

Perry Street

176 Perry Street (Corner of Perry Street and West Side Highway)

Perry Street

Address: 176 Perry Street, New York, NY 10014
(Corner of Perry Street and West Side Highway)
Phone: (212) 352-1900, *Fax:* (212) 352-1922
Internet: www.jean-georges.com

Cuisine: Contemporary American, French

Chef-Owner: Jean-Georges Vongerichten

Business hours: Lunch Monday-Friday: 12:00PM - 3:00PM
Dinner nightly: 5:30PM - 11:30PM - bar opens at 5:00PM
Brunch (Saturday and Sunday) 12:00PM - 3:00PM

General Manager: Seth Gurka

Executive Chef: Erik Battes

Pastry chef: Eric Hubert

Maître d'Hôtel: Jaeson Lee

Groups (max. group size): 10

Payment: Amex, Mastercard, Visa, Diners

Price: $60 And up per person

Food Ratings: 1 Michelin Star, 3 Stars New York Times

Reservations: Recommended

Dress Code: Casual

Interior Design: Thomas Juul-Hansen

From top left to bottom right:
- Japanese Snapper Sashimi, lemon, olive oil, and crispy skin
- Crispy Calamari, yuzu dipping sauce and sesame
- Arctic char, freshly squeezed cherry tomato juice,
  israeli couscous and cockles
- Chocolate pudding, fresh cream, crystallized violets

When two gastronomic enthusiasts meet …

Jeffrey Steingarten is a food critic for *Vogue* magazine. His articles are at once authoritative yet elegant, severe, provocative and witty. Residing in the gastronomic capital of the U.S., New York, Steingarten has all cuisines of the world close at hand. I called to ask him about developments in gastronomy today, especially in New York.

Jeffrey is a Harvard-trained lawyer who quit his job to become a food writer. In doing so he continues a grand tradition that started in France in the early 19th century when Jean-Anthelme Brillat-Savarin published his still-famous *La Phsiologie du Goût* (*The Physiology of Taste*). Brillat-Savarin was also a lawyer and his book can be considered the first on gastronomy. The book is just as humorous and convincing as Jeffrey's works. The 'Aphorisms of the Professor' are well-known, many of which apply to Steingarten, like "the Creator, while forcing men to eat in order to live, tempts him to do so with appetite and then rewards him with pleasure."

Steingarten's appetite must be insatiable – an indispensable asset to gastronomes. If he writes about foie gras, he finds that he'd "first have to eat lots more of it before taking a stab at writing about it." And immediately after he has landed in Memphis to get to know more about barbecue, he wants first "to visit the best barbecue place between the airport and his hotel. An hour or two later he visits the best barbecue place between his hotel and dinner. To continue in Memphis, where he finds making choices not easy, because there are so many barbecue restaurants to choose from".

In terms of cuisine, barbecue restaurants are popular in New York City these days. According to Steingarten, the real barbecue, not grilling, but cooking meats covered and at low temperature for long periods of time, is the most important contribution the U.S. has made to world cuisine. Other popular cuisines are the new but true hamburger restaurants and all types of Japanese restaurants. "Of all the cities I know outside of Japan, New York has the best Japanese food in the world," says Steingarten.

In terms of technique, restaurants serving "science food" are very trendy in New York. "It is ten times harder to get into one of these restaurants than to get enrolled at Harvard," Jeffrey states. In particular, low-temperature cooking is hot. How strange and annoying that *sous vide* is not allowed in most restaurants. *Sous vide* is vacuum-packing food in a plastic bag. Sometimes the food is cooked in the bag. Other times, the pressure of the packing process is used to infuse flavors into ingredients. In 2006, the New York City Health Department made the very successful David Chang of Momofuku destroy $1,500 of food that was being prepared this way.

Low temperature cooking is just one of the aspects of hypermodern food, as Steingarten likes to call it. Spain's Ferran Adrià closes his restaurant El Bulli for six months to develop new dishes, which are often based on new techniques, many of which require new machines, powders and gels. Steingarten takes a dim view on government opinions on food and health. Light versions of products are not what they promise to be. In fact they are often higher in calories than the true and original versions, based on natural sugar, fat or salt. Bad nutritional advice is something he just cannot tolerate. In the essay "Fear of Formaggio," for instance, he takes on lactose intolerance, saying that most cheeses that intolerants avoid have no lactose in them and that several studies show that many people who claim said intolerance are faking it. "Food paranoia has nearly destroyed both the genial dinner party and the warm family meal, and with them, our sense of festivity and exchange, of community and sacrament," according to Steingarten.

Jeffrey's best gastronomic experiences are when the food is perfectly prepared. But he finds that this is seldom the case. People often don't know or they just don't care or they simply don't use the good ingredients. The issue of the availability and importance of good ingredients is nowadays subject of an ongoing debate between chefs. Which is more important: ingredient or technique? Many of today's modern chefs will say technique. With the new tricks of the trade ingredients are turned into powders, foams and gels. Yet it bears remembering that a single focus on today's food magic will not last. If you go back to traditional French food, in times where hypermodern food, or science food, prevails, you realise how good it really was. Good ingredients are always the best start to good food.

Peter Klosse

Picholine
35 West 64th Street (Between Central Park West and Broadway)

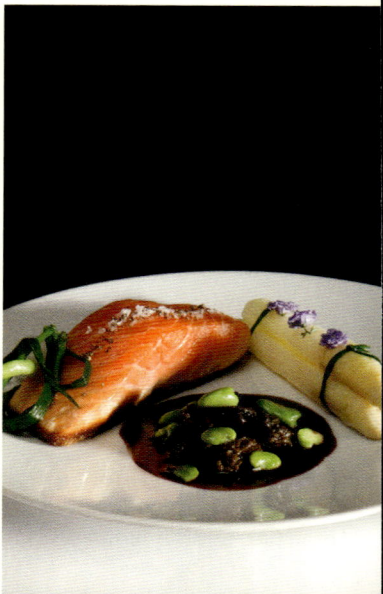

Picholine

Address: 35 West 64th Street, New York, NY 10023
(Between Central Park West and Broadway)
Phone: (212) 724 8585, *Fax:* (212) 875 8979
Internet: www.picholinenyc.com, *Email:* info@picholinenyc.com

Cuisine: Mediterranean

Chef-Owner: Terrance Brennan

Business hours: Mon-Thu 5:00PM - 10:00PM, Fri-Sat 5:00PM - 11:45PM
Sun 5:00PM - 9:00PM

GM-Sommelier: Jason Miller, *Chef de Cuisine:* Carmine DiGiovanni

Private dining: The Wine Room seats up to 8 and L'Olivier seats up to 22

Price: 3 courses $92, each additonal course $12

Payment: All major credit cards

Ratings: 2 Michelin Stars, Zagat: Food 27, Service 25
New York Times: 3 stars

Reservations: Recommended

Dress Code: Casual, Jackets recommended, no sneakers or shorts

Parking: Garage located across the street at ICON
Parking for Lincoln Center 24 hrs. / 7 days
1 Lincoln Plaza 1900-1916 Broadway (entrance on 63rd)

Additional Features: Store selling a.o. Artisanal Premium Cheese,
See website for classes and workshops

From top left to bottom right:
- Sausage and Egg
  A la Basquaise and Idiazabal Frico
- Tuna Cru "Napoleon"
  Flavors of the Riviera and Olive Oil Ice Cream
- Vermont Loin of Rabbit
  Fresh Tagliatelle, Ramps and Wild Snails
- Wild King Salmon
  Spring Onions, White Asparagus and Morels

Scalini Fedeli

165 Duane Street (Between Greenwich and Hudson Streets)

Scalini Fedeli

Address: 165 Duane Street, New York, NY 10013
(Between Greewich and Hudson Streets)
Phone: (212) 528 0400
Internet: www.scalinifedelinyc.com

Cuisine: Italian

Chef-Owner: Michael Cetrulo

Business hours: 12:00PM - 3:00PM, 5:30PM - 10:00PM,
Friday-Saturday 5:30PM - 11:00PM
closed Sun, No lunch on Monday

General Manager and Wine Steward: John Stantinos

Groups (max. group size): 10

Private dining: 20 seats in the wine cellar

Payment: Amex, Mastercard, Visa, Diners

Price: $70 and up per person

Ratings: 1 Michelin Star, Zagat: Food 26, Service 25

Reservations: Recommended, *Dress Code:* Business Casual

Interior Design: Vaulted ceiling with antique stained glass

From top left to bottom:
• Wild striped bass with a Sicilian olive-tomato jus and caponata with currants
• Hamachi "yellowtail" with oven roasted San Marzano tomatoes, zucchini
  and red peppers with a provencal vinaigrette and tapenade
• Arborio Risotto with artichoke, zucchini and asparagus finished with a veal
  and marsala wine glaze

A Star is Born: April Bloomfield

We go way back with April Bloomfield, the chef and owner of The Spotted Pig. April worked at The River Café in London with English chef Jamie Oliver, who has been our client for the past seven years. Before the Pig opened, April worked with us while Jamie was touring in San Francisco. She told us about her vision of a great neighborhood gastro-pub where New Yorkers could hang out and eat and drink some seriously good food in a casual atmosphere. We were excited, but a little worried too, because in New York after all, aren't there hundreds of other places like that already?

And we were worried about April, too. Sure she could cook, but how was a shy, Northern English girl going to take New York by storm? Even with the support of her star-power partners: super-connected ex-music executive, Ken Friedman, and Mario Batali - yes, Molto Mario., April had to command the kitchen and the critics all by herself.

We couldn't see how this 105-pound workaholic chef was going to make New Yorkers happy serving pints of Old Speckled Hen ale, a re-tuned River Café gnudi and one great burger. We couldn't have been more wrong.

In a kitchen no bigger than a walk-in closet, April and her boys got to work putting out food that was not only noticed by American critics, but was awarded one star from the Michelin Guide. One star for a small gastro-pub filled with pig paraphernalia shocked the food community around the world, and made April an overnight star.

After the Michelin star, we started seeing April in the dining room more. She now stops and visits with regulars at the few times a day where the restaurant isn't crowded. Unlike other chefs, when VIPs were in the house, April still leaves them to Ken while she goes back to the place where she's most comfortable: behind the stove.

It's a rare day that April isn't in The Pig, but that will change soon. In a small sliver of a location next to Del Posto, April and Ken are opening a English fish restaurant, to be called The John Dory. She's also in the process of writing her first cookbook, and was one of only two chefs to beat Iron Chef Michael Symon in a battle on Food Network.

April Bloomfield is now on her way to becoming a celebrity chef in her own right. We couldn't be prouder to say we knew her when.

Kimberly Yorio and Caitlin Friedman

For over 15 years, Kimberly Yorio has specialized in the development of strategic publicity and promotions campaigns for cookbooks, food-related personalities and products, chefs and restaurants.

After co-founding YC Media with Caitlin, Kim has driven campaigns ranging from the launch of Sur La Table's first store in Manhattan to the creation and promotion of the Beard Papa brand. Among the firm's talent clients, she has led the media efforts for Jamie Oliver and his last six cookbooks, as well as the launch of TLC's Take Home Chef, "Curtis Stone."

Caitlin Friedman is a public relations and marketing professional with more than fifteen years of consumer, food and beverage, publishing, and television-production experience.

As a partner in YC Media, Caitlin has led a variety of publicity efforts including the creation of "The American Chef," an events company centered around White House Executive Chef Walter Scheib, and the successful launch of the new concept, Vino Volo, a high-end chain of wine tasting lounges in airports.

The Spotted Pig
314 West 11th Street (On the corner of Greenwich Street)

The Spotted Pig

Address: 314 West 11th Street, New York, NY 10014
(On the corner of Greenwich Street)
Phone: (212) 620 0393, *Fax:* (212) 366 1666
Internet: www.thespottedpig.com

Cuisine: Seasonal British & Italian using local ingredients when possible.

Chef-Owner: April Bloomfield & Ken Friedman

Business hours: Brunch: 11:00AM - 3:00PM (weekends),
Lunch: 12:00PM - 3:00PM, Bar Menu: 3:00PM - 5:00PM,
Dinner: 5:30PM - 2:00AM

Closed: (Vacation) December 25th

Executive Chef: April Bloomfield

Groups (max. group size): 6

Private Dining: events@thespottedpig.com

Payment: All Major Credit Cards

Price: $40 and up per person

Food Ratings: 1 Michelin Star for 2005, 2006, 2007

Reservations: Not Accepted; Seating is on a walk-in basis only

Dress Code: No Dress Code

Interior Design: Ken Friedman

Additional features: April Bloomfield was selected as one of the Best New Chefs 2007 of Food & Wine Magazine. Recently, April Bloomfield won the battle of Iron Chef on The Food Network as a challenger. Parking can usually be found on street in the neighborhood. There is a parking lot across Greenwich Street and one on West 11th Street between Greenwich and Washington Streets.

From top left to bottom right:
- Roasted Asparagus with Parmesan Custard
- Monkfish Daube with Girolles & Potatoes
- Sheep's Ricotta Gnudi with Brown Butter & Sage
- Rhubarb tart

Go Green with Water?

Europeans have often blazed the way on the eco-movement, developing better approaches to waste and emissions. A product adapted from stylish European cafés, the Natura Water system, lets high-end restaurants purify local water to still or sparkling water for their customers. Is water the next aspiration in the greening of America?

In Europe, the value and quality of locally grown and raised foods, in season and impeccably prepared, are hallmarks of top meals and top chefs. "Local" and "in-season" are now buzzwords with American diners and restaurateurs. Besides enjoying produce tasting as it should, there are real economic, environmental and sustainability issues with choices made at the dining table. Europe does not share American issues with population and geography in going local, but we do share the same environmental concerns.

London and Stockholm have started efforts to ban bottled water from city-owned venues. Newly progressive city governments like New York and Los Angeles may not be far behind. Why? Recently, before a Senate sub-committee, the Natural Resources Defense Council testified that the process of manufacturing and transporting one liter of water actually consumes nine liters of water.

The carbon footprint of bottled water doesn't end with the processing and shipments into stores and restaurants. It's estimated about 80% of the almost 35 million plastic water bottles consumed every day end up getting trucked out to never decompose in landfills. With economic conditions and greater awareness, maybe bottled water consumption will decrease - and go green with local premium water.

Natura, www.naturawater.com

Sushi Yasuda
204 East 43rd Street (Between 2nd and 3rd Ave.)

Sushi Yasuda

Address: 204 East 43rd Street, New York, NY 10017
(Between 2nd and 3rd Avenues)
Phone: (212) 972 1001, *Fax:* (212) 972 1717
Internet: sushiyasuda.com

Cuisine: sushi

Chef-Owner: Naomichi Yasuda

Business hours: Lunch: Monday - Friday, 12:00PM - 2:15PM;
Dinner: Monday - Saturday, 6:00PM - 10:15PM

Closed: (Vacation) Sundays and National holidays

General Manager-Owner: Shige Akimoto

Designer/Marketing/Concept-Owner: Scott Rosenberg

Groups (max. group size): 6

Private Dining: NA

Payment: Amex, Mastercard, Visa, Diners

Price: $50 and up per person

Food Ratings: 28 (Number 2 overall in NYC) Zagat, Food,
3 stars New York Times

Reservations: strongly suggested

Dress Code: business casual

Architecture: clean Japanese modern

Interior Design: solid bamboo hardwood surfaces - walls, floors ceilings

From top to bottom
- Bluefin Tuna, Bluefin Fatty Tuna, Fluke, Hiramasa Yellowtail
  Tasmanian Sea Trout, White King Salmon
- Tuna Rolls, Sanma, Kobashira, Sea Urchin

Buttermilk

When it's summer and the heat is rising from the sidewalks, and you've been cycling for ages, there are two things you can do: you can drink an ice cold beer, freshly tapped, or you can pour yourself a stone cold glass of buttermilk. Alas, buttermilk is 'not done' in trendy settings. We need to mount a protest against this travesty, and label restaurants that don't serve buttermilk as blasé.

Everyone should drink this nectar of the gods with a repast of whiting or codfish, fennel, sautéed onion and crispy bacon.
Buttermilk is what is left after churning milk. Because the milkfat is churned out, the milk that is left tastes sour. This milk contains many vitamins and it is bursting with minerals. In the United Kingdom they make scones with buttermilk. These are delicious with clotted cream and marmelade. Once upon a time, we used to get buttermilk porridge with syrup for breakfast. Oh yes, once upon a time, but then sometimes, in those days, it wasn't such a mouth watering treat.

Will Jansen

Will Jansen is a well-known Dutch food writer, with more than 10 books to his name. He is also the distributor and the editor-in-chief of Bouillon, a gastronomic quarterly full of reports, stories and tales about the world of restaurants, food and drinks, twice awarded the Gourmand World Cook Book Award. He has done interviews with a greater part of the European three-star Michelin chefs like Alain Ducasse, Nadia Santini, Jonnie Boer, Pierre Gagnaire, Ferran Adria, but also American chefs like Thomas Keller, Charly Trotter and Testuya Wakuda.

Very healthy rhubarb

Who still eats rhubarb? Not many, I'll wager. Too sour, too sharp. Most people don't know how to make something tasty of it. The Dutch discovered rhubarb in the sixteenth century, but it is much older than that. It grew in Siberia five thousand years ago. From there, it went to China. The Greeks called it rha barbaron (that which was brought by the barbarians from across the Volga River), and used it medicinally. Rhubarb root contains antrachinon, an extremely effective laxative, and the malic acid in the stalks is purifying for the blood. Hollanders also used this plant medicinally, and it was a mere three hundred years ago that it turned up in cookbooks, thanks to the British.

Eat the young stalks, that's what the experts usually say, and prepare it with sugar, honey, ginger or cinnamon to temper the tartness. Rhubarb pie is delicious, but mix the fruit filling with an equal amount of apple, preferably goudrenette, to temper the bitterness. Rhubarb pie is an excellent follow-up to a heavy meal.

Will Jansen

Tocqueville
1 East 15th Street (between 5th Avenue and Union Square)

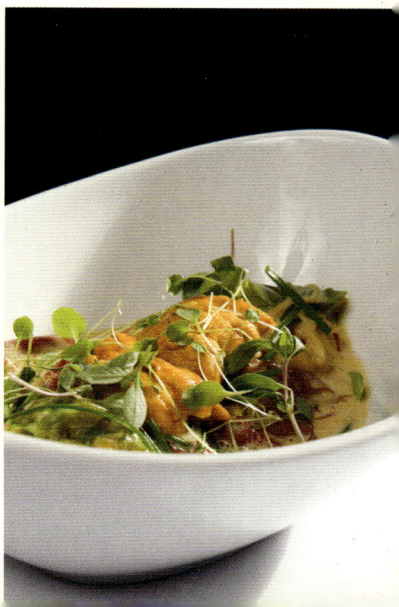

Tocqueville

Address: 1 East 15th Street, New York, NY 10003
(Between 5th and Union Square)
Phone: (212) 647 1515
Internet: www.tocquevillerestaurant.com

Cuisine: French American

Owners: Jo-Ann Makovitzky and Marco Moreira

Business hours: 11:45AM - 2:00PM, 5:30PM - 10:30PM
Closed Sun.

General Manager: Jo-Ann Makovitzky

Executive Chef: Marco Moreira

Chef de Cuisine: David Coleman

Pastry Chef: Danny Martinez

Sommeliers: Vittorio Peluso and Nick Robinson

Groups (max. group size): 74 sit down

Payment: Amex, Mastercard, Visa, Diners

Price: Prix Fixe Lunch $ 24, 3 Course Greenmarket Lunch and Dinner $48

Ratings: Zagat: Food 26, Service 25

Reservations: recommended

Dress Code: Business Casual

Interior Design: Alexandra Champalimaud

Additional features: Handicap Accessible, Catering, Greenmarket Menus
from Memorial Day to Columbus Day, Prix Fixe Lunch, Pre Theater

From top left to bottom:
- Green and White Asparagus Salad with Truffle Vinaigrette and Herb Salad
- Frozen Tangerine Soufflé, Citrus Salad and Black Tea Sorbet
- Dry-Aged Salt-Crusted Ribeye of Beef, Bone Marrow Flan, Glazed Ramp Bulbs, Forest Mushrooms and Farofa
- California Sea Urchin and Angel Hair Carbonara

Veritas

43 East 20th Street (Between Broadway and Park Avenue South)

Veritas

Address: 43 East 20th Street, New York, NY 10003
(Between Broadway and Park Ave South)
Phone: (212) 353 3700, *Fax:* (212) 353 1632
Internet: www.veritas-nyc.com

Cuisine: Contemporary French

Business hours: Mon-Sat 5:30PM - 11:00PM, Sunday 5:00PM - 10:00PM

Closed: (Vacation) No

General Manager: Tim Bellardo

Executive Chef: Gregory Pugin

Pastry chef: Meena Pizarro

Maître d'Hôtel: Tim Bellardo

Wine Steward: Tim Kopec Wine Director

Groups (max. group size): 8

Private Dining: no

Payment: Amex, Mastercard, Visa, Diners

Price: $90 prix fix per person

Food Ratings: 1 Michelin Star, 27 Zagat, Food, 3 Stars New York Times

Service Ratings: 26 out of 30

Reservations: Suggested

Dress Code: Casual

From top left to bottom:
- Foie Gras
  red wine poached, onion marmalade
- Dover Sole Provencal
  ratatouille, zucchini flowers, romesco sauce
- Summer Market Salad
  tuna belly confit

Vong

200 East 54th Street (Southeast Corner of 3rd Avenue)

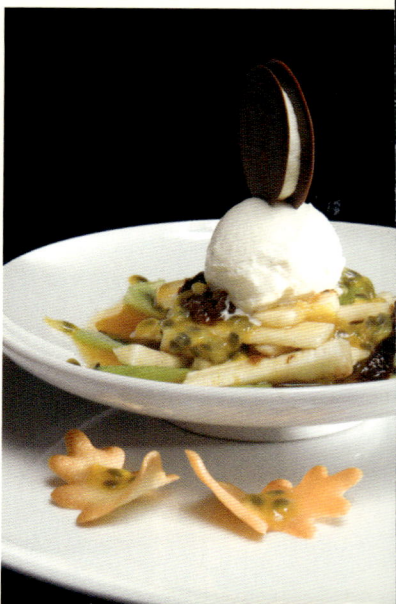

Vong

Address: 200 East 54th Street, New York, NY 10022
(southeast corner of 3rd Ave in the Lipstick Building)
Phone: (212) 486 9592, *Fax:* (212) 980 3745
Internet: www.jean-georges.com

Cuisine: French/Thai Fusion

Chef-Owner: Jean-Georges Vongerichten

Business hours: 12:00PM - 3:00PM Saturday and Sunday no lunch,
5:30PM - 11:00PM, Saturday 5:00PM - 11:00PM,
Sunday 5:30PM - 10:00PM

General Manager: Christian Amestoy

Executive Chef: Pierre Schutz, *Pastry chef:* Eric Hubert

Wine Steward: Carrie Lyn Strong

Groups (max. group size): 8, *Private Dining:* No, semi-private only

Payment: American Express, Visa, MasterCard, Diner's Club, Discover, JCB

Price: $55 And up per person

Food Ratings: 1 Michelin Star, Zagat Food: 22, Service: 23,
3 Stars New York Times

Reservations: Recommended, *Dress Code:* Casual

Architecture: David Rockwell, *Interior Design:* David Rockwell

Additional features: Parking available on 54th street

From top left to bottom right:
• The tasting plate
• Duck breast, spicy tamarind and sesame sauce
• Passion fruit soufflé, passion fruit ice cream
• Exotic fruit salad, white pepper ice cream

The salt of the earth

"I have noticed," exclaimed the late Bernard Loiseau (Michelin three-star chef who took his own life), "that the average amateur chef doesn't know how to salt his/her dishes. They strew a little here, strew a little there, or wave the salt shaker around a bit. Wrong!

The first rule of proper salting is: put your salt into a salt cellar so you can use it by the pinch, and return what you don't need to the cellar.

Rule two: hold your plate or pan at eye level so you can see how much salt you are actually using.

Rule three: Use 20 grams of salt to one liter of water when cooking vegetables. That means no more than one tablespoon!

Rule four: Never salt your meat before putting it in the pan! Salt pulls the moisture away from the center of the meat, making it much less tender.

Rule five: Salt your fish halfway through the cooking process. If you do it sooner, the fish will stick to the pan, and that is no easy problem to solve. Sea salt from Guérande is the best salt variety for cooking vegetables or making bouillon. Salt your fish, chicken, meat and sauces with fine salt.

Will Jansen

Fast food more expensive than three-star cuisine

As a staff writer for a Rotterdam magazine, I was given the task of writing an article comparing two very different restaurants: Burger King and the Michelin three-star Parkheuvel, where Cees Helder was currently head chef. Apart from all of the obvious differences - the battalion of kow-towing friendliness versus security cameras as hearty welcome - it struck me that fast food is actually quite expensive.

The whole idea of "fast" makes one's costs-per-minute disproportionately high. To demonstrate: 15 minutes at a Burger King for salad, hamburger menu, microwaved brownie and a dirty bathroom cost me $ 14.25. This is $ 57.00 per hour. At Parkheuvel, King Cees charged $ 90,25 for a savory two hours that included a three-course lunch and three glasses of house wine. The culinary rate per hour for this meal was $ 45.00. That is a good $ 12.00 per hour cheaper than Burger King.

He who dines at fine restaurants can consider himself a savvy businessman.

Maarten van der Jagt

Wallse
344 West 11th Street (corner of Washington Street)

Wallse

Address: 344 West 11th Street (corner of Washington Street)
New York, NY 10014
Phone: (212) 352 2300
Internet: www.kg-ny.com

Cuisine: Modern interpretation of classical Viennese cuisine

Chef-Owner: Chef Kurt Gutenbrunner

Business hours: 5:30PM - 11:00PM, Brunch at Sun & Sat 11.00AM - 02:30PM

Closed: (Vacation) Christmas Eve and Christmas Day

General Manager: Christopher Ardu

Executive Chef: Kurt Gutenbrunner, *Sous Chef:* Connie Quehenberger

Pastry chef: Matthew Lodes, *Wine Steward:* Christopher Ardu

Groups (max. group size): 8

Private Dining: 75 seats for entire space or 40 seats for the one room.

Payment: Amex, Mastercard, Visa, Diners

Price: About $55 per person (not including beverages)

Ratings: 1 Michelin Star, 2 Stars from the NY Times, Zagat: Food 26, Service 23

Reservations: Highly Recommended, … Casual chic

Architecture: Constantin Wickenburg Architects

Design: Artist/filmmaker Julian Schnabel, including three of his own paintings. Also featuring pieces by Alfred Oehlen, Martin Kippenberger, Alejandro Garmendia, and Dennis Hopper.

Additional features: Outdoor seating available, dining at the bar, wine pairing menus available.

From top left to bottom right:
• Florida Shrimp with watermelon and watercress
• Long Island Wild Striped bass with zucchini, eggplant caviar, and purple olives
• "Sacher Torte," raspberry ragout and chocolate cream
• Sour cream panna cotta with rhubarb and strawberries

wd~50

50 Clinton Street (Between Rivington and Stanton)

wd~50

Address: 50 Clinton Street, New York, NY 10002
(Between Rivington and Stanton)
Phone: (212) 477 2900
Internet: www.wd-50.com

Cuisine: Modern American

Owners: Wylie Dufresne, Jean-Goerges Vongerichten and Philip Suarez

Business hours: 6.00PM - 11.00PM, on Sunday 6.00PM - 10.00PM

Closed: Thanksgiving Day, Christmas Day, New Years Day

Chef: Wylie Dufresne, *Sous chef:* Kevin Heston

Pastry chef: Alex Stupak

Maître d'Hotel: Geoffrey Fischer

Wine Stewards: Dewey Dufresne

Groups (max. group size): 8

Private dining: In the Wine Cellar up to 14 guests

Payment: All Major cards excepted

Price: $75 and up per person

Ratings: 1 Michelin Star, Zagat: Food 23, Service 25, NY Times: 3 stars

Reservations: Encouraged, *Dress Code:* Casual Chic

Interior Design: Fireplace and lighting by Louis Mueller

Notable features: cocktails reflect the cuisine

From top left to bottom right:
- Popcorn soup, shrimp, jicama, tamarind
- Cherry covered chocolate, molasses, lime
- Wagyu flat iron, coffee gnocchi,coconut, cipollini, sylvetta
- Knot foie

Index culinaria by title